PRENTICE-HALL   ✓ **W9-DAT-755**
FOUNDATIONS OF MODERN SOCIOLOGY SERIES

Alex Inkeles, Editor

THE SCIENTIST'S ROLE IN SOCIETY
Joseph Ben-David

DEVIANCE AND CONTROL
Albert K. Cohen

MODERN ORGANIZATIONS
Amitai Etzioni

SOCIAL PROBLEMS
Amitai Etzioni

THE FAMILY
William J. Goode

SOCIETY AND POPULATION, Second Edition
David M. Heer

WHAT IS SOCIOLOGY? An Introduction to the Discipline and Profession
Alex Inkeles

THE SOCIOLOGY OF SMALL GROUPS
Theodore M. Mills

SOCIAL CHANGE, Second Edition
Wilbert E. Moore

THE SOCIOLOGY OF RELIGION
Thomas F. O'Dea

SOCIETIES: Evolutionary and Comparative Perspectives
Talcott Parsons

THE SYSTEM OF MODERN SOCIETIES
Talcott Parsons

THE AMERICAN SCHOOL: A Sociological Analysis
Patricia C. Sexton

THE SOCIOLOGY OF ECONOMIC LIFE, Second Edition
Neil J. Smelser

FOUNDATIONS OF MODERN SOCIOLOGY
Metta Spencer

SOCIAL STRATIFICATION: The Forms and Functions of Inequality
Melvin M. Tumin

Foundations of Modern Sociology Series

the sociology
of small groups

Theodore M. Mills, *Yale University*

Prentice-Hall, Inc., *Englewood Cliffs, New Jersey*

To Mary Jane

Prentice-Hall Foundations of Modern Sociology Series

Alex Inkeles, *Editor*

Current printing (last digit):
18   17   16   15   14

PRENTICE-HALL INTERNATIONAL, INC., *London*
PRENTICE-HALL OF AUSTRALIA, PTY., LTD., *Sydney*
PRENTICE-HALL OF CANADA, LTD., *Toronto*
PRENTICE-HALL OF INDIA PRIVATE LIMITED, *New Delhi*
PRENTICE-HALL OF JAPAN, INC., *Tokyo*

C

acknowledgments

I wish to thank Robert N. Bellah, François Bourricaud, Donald R. Matthews, Luciano Gallino, and William P. Yohe, my colleagues at the Center for Advanced Study in the Behavorial Sciences, for fruitful discussions on modern sociological theory from which this book benefits; graduate students in the Department of Sociology, Yale University, too numerous to list but including Peter J. Burke and Michael Farrell, whose dual concern for relevance and clarity helped define the book's emphasis; Philip E. Slater, J. Zvi Namenwirth, and George Huaco, for critical reviews of selected chapters; and Anna Tower (of the Center), Mary Elizabeth Hintze, and Nora C. Quiocho, for their assistance in typing and for suggested improvements in exposition. I am especially grateful to Alex Inkeles, General Editor of Prentice-Hall's Foundations of Modern Sociology Series, for his criticism and suggestions during the book's early stages and for his patience and support throughout a later period of formulation and reformulation.

contents

vii

introduction

Most branches of social science have expanded rapidly since World War II. New interest, new talent, new skills, new resources, and a new confidence, along with a new receptivity to what is being learned, have combined in a broadly based—perhaps revolutionary—trend on the part of man to learn more about himself through the mode of scientific inquiry. Even taking this general trend into account, the recent increase in research and thought on the small human group has been remarkable.[1]

A visit to almost any library would demonstrate that since the early forties the number of journal articles on the small human group has increased at a geometric rate, and in the same vein a general tour of universities would show that courses on groups have been added, new laboratories for small-group research have been built, and the number of investigators conducting research both in the community and in the laboratory has increased tremendously. Nor has this growth been restricted to a single academic field: it has occurred throughout the social sciences, including psychology, social psychology, psychiatry, sociology, political science, and anthropology, as well as in the related fields of applied mathematics, cybernetics, and general system theory. In other words,

---

[1] For reviews of the development of the field, see Fred L. Strodtbeck and A. Paul Hare, "Bibliography of Small Group Research: 1900 through 1953," *Sociometry* (1954), XVII: 107–178; Edgar F. Borgatta, "Small Group Research," *Current Sociology* (1960), IX: 173–200.

1

investigators in many fields are directing their attention to what happens among persons when they meet at close range; they are seeking a new understanding of the dynamics of small groups.

Before we go any further, let us consider the question which no doubt is already on the mind of the reader: Just what *are* these small groups we are referring to? To put it simply, they are *units composed of two or more persons who come into contact for a purpose and who consider the contact meaningful.* Some of these groups—families, for instance—are relatively separate, while others, like boards of directors, are parts of larger units. Other examples might be construction gangs, hunting parties, town committees, ceremonial dance teams, bomber crews, athletic teams. To say simply that there are many more is to understate the case. The fact is, that with some 3,200,000,000-plus individuals in the world, each one belonging to an average of five or six groups, and allowing for overlap, an estimate of the total number of small groups now existing runs as high as four to five billion. (Since in any given community a number of individuals are likely to belong to some of the same groups, the total number of groups is less than the total number of memberships. Still, because each individual belongs, as we say, to an average of from five to six groups, the total number of groups is considerably greater than the total number of individuals.) Add to these all past and future groups, and the figure swells into the many billions.

Why Study Small Groups?

Granted that the great number of small groups is surprising—but why should we study them? The first reason is pragmatic. We need to understand what happens within such groups, both because their decisions have a critical effect upon the history of communities, and because their dynamics affect the way individuals lead their daily lives. We already know such things as how a handful of leaders commit their nation to a course of action, and how widely-distributed decisions made in private by millions of married couples (to continue to have babies) can contribute to the population explosion. And we know, too, that the groups which surround the individual in his daily life not only are sources of respect, affection, and protection, but also are causes of strain, cross-pressures, conflict, and frustration. We need to know far more, for greater knowledge of group dynamics can help the individual to better manage his all-important group life.[2]

The second reason for studying small groups is social-psychological. Because social pressures and pressures from the individual meet in the small group, it is a convenient context in which to observe and to experiment on the interplay among these pressures. Scientific investigation may lead to general laws about how individuals cope with social realities.[3]

The third reason is sociological. The direct task is to understand small groups in their own right and to create empirically-based theories about the dynamics of these many billions of transitory systems, much as the task of physiology is to formulate working theories of the dynamics of transitory living organisms.

The fourth reason is more ambitious. Small groups are a special case of

---

[2] Warren G. Bennis, Kenneth D. Benne and Robert Chin (eds.), *The Planning of Change* (New York: Holt, Rinehart and Winston, 1961).

[3] Robert E. L. Faris, "Development of the Small Group Research Movement," in Muzafer Sherif and M. O. Wilson (eds.), *Group Relations at the Crossroads* (New York: Harper, 1953), pp. 155–184.

2

the more general type of system, the social system. Not only are they micro-systems, they are essentially microcosms of larger societies. They present, in miniature, societal features, such as division of labor, a code of ethics, a government, media of exchange, prestige rankings, ideologies, myths, and religious practices. Through careful examination of these microsystems, theoretical models can be constructed and then applied to less accessible societies for further test and modification. Small-group research is thus a means of developing effective ways of thinking about social systems in general.[4]

A Short History
of the Study of Small Groups

Scientific study of groups is largely a twentieth-century phenomenon; earlier nineteenth-century sociologists were understandably preoccupied with major historical trends.[5] Given the newly emerging capitalist societies and bureaucratic states, the formation of new class structures and the dissolution of the intimate groupings in the traditional community, attention was drawn more to what was forming than to what was breaking up—and a dichotomy existed between the dislodged individual and the large system. It is true that Durkheim appreciated the importance of primary group ties in the operation of both social [6] and personal control [7] and that Simmel conceived of the mutuality in social relations,[8] yet these were exceptions: small groupings were overlooked and the dichotomy remained. The new psychology dealt with the individual, the new sociology with the total society.

Partly in response to this gap, Cooley, in the United States, emphasized the affinity between the person and the group: the infant savage becomes social through intimate and prolonged interaction in the primary family group; [9] throughout life, close ties with other persons sustain the individual, stabilize his thought, and give him a sense of direction. Cooley noted the ease with which the boundaries between the individual and group are magnified, and the difficulty in recognizing the connections between them. Such connections were demonstrated in the work of Thomas, who showed that when groups disintegrate, the psyche of persons attached to them tends to disintegrate,[10] and in

[4] Robert F. Bales, "The Equilibrium Problem in Small Groups," in Talcott Parsons, Robert F. Bales, and Edward A. Shils, *Working Papers in The Theory of Action* (New York: The Free Press of Glencoe, 1953), pp. 111–161. For comments on the strategy and function of small group research see Lewis A. Coser, "The Functions of Small Group Research," *Social Problems* (Winter 1955–1956), III: 1–6; Edgar F. Borgatta and Leonard S. Cottrell, "Directions for Research in Group Behavior," *American Journal of Sociology* (1957), LXIII: 42–48; and Alan P. Bates and N. Babchuck, "The Primary Group: A Reappraisal," *Sociological Quarterly* (July 1961), III: 181–191.

[5] For a perceptive interpretation of origins and trends see Edward A. Shils, "The Study of the Primary Group," in Daniel Lerner and Harold Lasswell (eds.), *The Policy Sciences* (Stanford: Stanford University Press, 1951), pp. 41–69.

[6] Emile Durkheim, *The Division of Labor*, trans. George Simpson (New York: The Free Press of Glencoe, 1933), especially pp. 1–31.

[7] Emile Durkheim, *Suicide*, trans. John A. Spaulding and George Simpson (New York: The Free Press of Glencoe, 1951), pp. 241–326.

[8] Kurt H. Wolff, *The Sociology of Georg Simmel* (New York: The Free Press of Glencoe, 1950), pp. 379–408; see also Georg Simmel, *Conflict: The Web of Group Affiliations*, trans. Kurt H. Wolff and Reinhard Bendix, respectively (New York: The Free Press of Glencoe, 1955), pp. 125–195.

[9] Charles H. Cooley, *Social Organization, A Study of the Larger Mind* (New York: Scribners, 1909).

[10] W. I. Thomas and Florian Znaniecki, *The Polish Peasant in Europe and America*, Vols. I–IV (Chicago: University of Chicago Press, 1918).

3

the work of Thrasher, who found that delinquent gangs train their recruits to crime, gain their loyalty, and protect them against society.[11] (This type of criminal behavior is as much a *group* phenomenon as an *individual* one.)

Meanwhile, the group's effect upon individuals was being discovered by experimentalists and by physicians. Moede in Germany found that racing cyclists went faster when they had a pacer;[12] F. H. Allport in the United States found that the presence of others facilitated superior task performance;[13] and Sherif found that persons who lack a secure basis for judging reality tend to adjust their perceptions toward the group's definition of that reality.[14]

The therapeutic effect of groups was discovered (in Boston), quite by accident, by Pratt, who noted that his deeply discouraged tuberculosis patients gave each other a kind of aid in discussions about their problems that he could not provide professionally.[15]

Before long, important advances were made to well beyond the point of merely recognizing that "groups made a difference." Industrial output, Mayo found, was materially affected by the network of group relations among workers:[16] not only did the workers fit their output to the standards of the informal team, but their identification with the company, their sense of being part of the larger unit, depended upon close primary relations of respect and affiliation between agents of the company and the informal team. Primary ties linked the single individual, the team, and the company. Later field work affirmed the fruitfulness of Mayo's formulation. For one thing, research showed that the fighting man in World War II found his strength and security through loyalty to his immediate comrades. His motivation to fight was local: he could not let his buddies down. For another, the coordination required to carry out the missions of a mammoth military organization was seen to depend in essence upon an overlapping network of primary personal ties.[17]

Meanwhile, Moreno, who sought to alter social arrangements in working groups to coincide more closely with the feelings and desires of members, invented a technique which has proven enormously useful to sociology.[18] He simply asked members to report to him how they felt about other members, whom they liked, whom they did not, those they wanted to work with, those with whom they did not. The device tapped the important dimension of the emotional relations among members and made it easy to chart and to compare patterns of these relations. Researchers quickly adopted the method and now use it extensively.

[11] Frederic Thrasher, *The Gang* (Chicago: University of Chicago Press, 1927).

[12] Walther Moede, "Der wetteifer, seine struktur und sein ausmass," *Z. päd. Psychol.* (1914), XV: 353–393; also see his *Experimentelle massenpsychologie* (Leipzig: Heizel, 1920).

[13] Floyd H. Allport, *Social Psychology* (Boston: Houghton Mifflin, 1924).

[14] Muzafer Sherif, "A Study of Some Social Factors in Perception," *Archives of Psychology* (1935), XXVII; also see his *The Psychology of Social Norms* (New York: Harper, 1936).

[15] For a brief review of the origins of treatment in groups see Max Rosenbaum and Milton Berger (eds.), *Group Psychotherapy and Group Function* (New York: Basic Books, 1963), pp. 3–22.

[16] Elton Mayo, *The Human Problems of an Industrial Civilization* (New York: Macmillan, 1933); see also the work of his associates in F. J. Rothlisberger and W. J. Dickson, *Management and the Worker: Technical vs. Social Organization in an Industrial Plant* (Cambridge: Harvard University Press, 1939).

[17] Edward A. Shils, "Primary Groups in the American Army," in Robert K. Merton and Paul F. Lazarsfeld (eds.), *Continuities in Social Research: Studies in The Scope and Method of "The American Soldier"* (New York: The Free Press of Glencoe, 1950), pp. 16–39.

[18] Jacob L. Moreno, "Sociometry and the Cultural Order," *Sociometry* (1943), VI: 299–344; and Jacob L. Moreno, *Who Shall Survive?*, rev. ed. (Beacon, N. Y.: Beacon House, 1953).

introduction

A new direction was given the study of groups by Kurt Lewin, who envisioned a more vigorous use of the experimental method in social science.[19] Social behavior, he asserted, is lawful; its laws are to be found through knowledge of the field of psychological and social forces which at any moment serve as causes of behavior. The science of groups depends upon locating and measuring these forces. One technique is to create different groups with known characteristics, then observe their operation. One can, for instance, set up groups under different styles of leaders, observe how the leaders act, how the members respond, compare the results, and then draw empirically based conclusions about the dynamic effects of leadership. Through these and other simple yet scientifically sound procedures, theoretically relevant hypotheses can be tested in the experimental laboratory.

Lewin attracted a generation of able social scientists. Deutsch tested the differential effects of cooperation and competition upon groups;[20] Bavelas artificially controlled who in the group could send information to whom, and tested the effects of such communication networks on group efficiency and satisfaction;[21] and Festinger, Schachter, and Bach tested the effects of group cohesion upon pressures to conform to group norms.[22] A predominant (though not exclusive) theme in post-Lewinian experimental research has been the classical social-psychological question of the group's effect upon the single member.

More distinctly sociological conceptions were presented in the early fifties, particularly in the work of Bales. In close contact with Parsons and Shils and influenced by their conceptual scheme in *Toward a General Theory of Action*,[23] Bales presented a sociological theory of group interaction, and an empirical scoring technique to go with it.[24] Groups as miniature social systems confront the standard system problems, such as how to adapt to the realities of the immediate situation, how to accomplish the group's goal, how to hold the group together, and how to satisfy members' needs. Groups must address themselves to these problems if they are to operate at all over a period of time. Since most interaction among members represents attempts to resolve system problems, one may classify each act according to the problem to which it is addressed. While groups vary in their cultures, they all confront a similar set of problems, and consequently, problem-oriented categories may be used universally. By applying a standard method of classifying interaction over a wide range of

[19] Kurt Lewin, "Frontiers in Group Dynamics," *Human Relations* (1947), I: 5–41; Kurt Lewin, "Frontiers in Group Dynamics: II," *Human Relations* (1947), I: 143–153; and Kurt Lewin and R. Lippitt, "An Experimental Approach to the Study of Autocracy and Democracy: A Preliminary Note," *Sociometry* (1938), I: 292–300.

[20] Morton Deutsch, "An Experimental Study of the Effects of Cooperation and Competition Upon Group Process," *Human Relations* (1949), II: 129–152, 199–231.

[21] Alex Bavelas, "Communication Patterns in Task-Oriented Groups," *Journal of the Acoustical Society of America* (1950), XX: 725–730, reprinted in Dorwin Cartwright and Alvin Zander (eds.), *Group Dynamics*, 2nd ed. (Evanston: Row, Peterson, 1960), pp. 669–682; for a follow-through study see Harold J. Leavitt, "Some Effects of Certain Communication Patterns on Group Performance," *Journal of Abnormal and Social Psychology* (1951), XLVI: 38–50, reprinted in Guy E. Swanson, Theodore M. Newcomb, and Eugene L. Hartley (eds.), *Readings in Social Psychology*, rev. ed. (New York: Holt, 1952).

[22] Leon Festinger, Stanley Schachter, and Kurt W. Bach, *Social Pressures in Informal Groups: A Study of Human Factors in Housing* (New York: Harper, 1950); see also Stanley Schachter, "Deviation Rejection and Communication," *Journal of Abnormal and Social Psychology* (1951), XLVI: 190–207, reprinted in Cartwright and Zander (eds.), *Group Dynamics*, 2nd ed., pp. 260–285.

[23] Talcott Parsons and Edward A. Shils (eds.), *Toward a General Theory of Action* (Cambridge: Harvard University Press, 1951).

[24] Robert F. Bales, *Interaction Process Analysis: A Method for the Study of Small Groups* (Reading, Mass.: Addison-Wesley, 1950).

5

groups, one can discover universal responses to system problems, including trends from the beginning to the end of a meeting, tendencies for members to divide their labor, and how attempts to resolve one problem complicates others.

The importance of Bales' approach is that it shifts attention from the group's effect on people and the situation to the effects of such variables upon the group: group processes themselves are the phenomena to be accounted for and explained. How do variables such as group size, personalities of members, emotional attachments, and so on affect the interaction process? What laws explain the process we observe? What laws explain the observable interaction throughout all small groups? Do the same laws hold for societies as well? The simplicity of Bales' technique has led to its wide use as a standard research method. It has also led to the development of supplementary methods to tap additional dimensions of group process, such as the content of what is being said and the emotional orientation of members toward others.

Conceiving of the group as a type of social system, as do Parsons and Bales, helped investigators think both in more abstract and in more general terms than previously; and experience in studying the act-by-act process among members in groups encouraged them to think in dynamic terms. These factors combined with others to stimulate new interest in formulating dynamic mathematical models of group processes. Although the idea of expressing complex system processes in mathematical terms is, of course, borrowed from physical scientists, it seems appropriate to social processes and, in fact, has become one of the exciting current trends in the field of small groups.[25]

Another important development, growing out of a renewed interest in emotional and symbolic processes, is the self-analytic group, the unique purpose of which is to understand group dynamics through exploring its own processes (rather than being studied by outsiders, it is studied by the members themselves). Historically, this is an outgrowth of group therapy and the work of Burrow, who in the 1920's presented a rationale for group therapy:[26] emotional disorders are due to unresolved problems occurring in a network of interpersonal relations; knowledge about them can be gained better when the patient is interacting with a variety of persons than in the traditional, one-to-one doctor-patient relationship; the patient's distorted view of himself is reflected through many eyes, and his confused ways of dealing with others are brought to light and clarified. But Burrow's argument was not well received, and group therapy lay dormant until World War II.

Heavy wartime demand, coupled with shortages of psychiatrists, forced group treatment, and finally the time came when physicians, especially several in England and in the United States,[27] began to realize some of the possibilities

[25] For a mathematical formulation of the theoretical system of George C. Homans in *The Human Group* (New York: Harcourt, Brace, 1950), see Herbert A. Simon, "A Formal Theory of Interaction in Social Groups," *American Sociological Review* (April 1952), XVII: 202–211; for more recent examples of mathematical treatment see Joan Criswell, Herbert Solomon, and Patric Suppes (eds.), *Mathematical Methods in Small Group Processes* (Stanford: Stanford University Press, 1962); and Joseph Berger, Bernard Cohen, J. Laurie Snell, and Morris Zelditch, Jr., *Types of Formalization in Small Group Research* (Boston: Houghton Mifflin, 1962).

[26] Trigant L. Burrow, "The Group Method of Analysis," *Psychoanalytic Review* (1924), XIV: 268–280.

[27] See W. R. Bion, *Experience in Groups, and Other Papers* (New York: Basic Books, 1959); S. H. Foulkes, *Introduction to Group-Analytic Psychotherapy* (London: Heineman Medical Books, 1948); Alexander Wolf, "The Psychoanalysis of Groups," *American Journal of Psychotherapy* (1949), 15–50 and (1950), 525–558; and J. Mann and Elvin V. Semrad, "Notes on the Use of Group Therapy in Psychosis," *Journal of Social Casework* (1948), 176–181.

6

of this new type of therapy. In practice, however, it soon became apparent that when patients meet together, they do more than simply present their "interpersonal past." Under the protection of the therapist, they draw together and create a new primary group, with its own code and structure and they tend to value their group, feel loyal to it, and identify with it. Clearly, if the therapist is to understand the individual patient in these circumstances, then he must comprehend the group and its effect upon the patient, too. In short, he must become a student of group dynamics.

One means of becoming a student of group dynamics is to set up a special type of group which examines itself. At Harvard University, Semrad conducted seminars wherein medical students and young social scientists met together, observed their own interaction, and interpreted to each other what the group was doing.[28] Although a simple enough arrangement, it is becoming increasingly apparent that such groups are a revolutionary departure, in the sense that they are a new order of social system. The collective purpose of their members is to learn about their collective experience. Goals preoccupying other groups are set aside so the group is free to develop an awareness of itself, to discover what its "self" is, where "self" means the group. Such groups have a built-in potential for becoming self-aware, self-knowing social systems, and consequently, of being a new order among social systems.

Not only do these groups draw attention to the more latent currents in the interpersonal situation and to the need for systematic methods for assessing them; they also provide participants with an immediate, pragmatic experience against which to judge myths and folk-beliefs about groups. Such knowledge instills confidence. Reinforced by other research and experimentation, this confidence has led to a remarkable proliferation of attempts to explore groups more deeply and to apply our knowledge about them more freely.

We would find these attempts illustrated concretely were we to make a tour of universities and laboratories. At Bethel, Maine, we find summer training laboratories where business executives, scientists, teachers, and others are gaining firsthand experience in group dynamics.[29] Elsewhere, at a west coast university we find groups of college students being given one frustrating task after the other in an experiment both to determine whether women exclude weak members as readily as men do, and to learn how they respond to very strong members. On another campus a group of resident psychiatrists are meeting to try to understand why their own group operates the way it does. At an east coast laboratory we find a mother, father, and their two teenage children jointly interpreting an ink blot. The investigator tells us that they have done a similar task in their livingroom at home, and that he is now observing how the relations among family members change as they enter the scientific laboratory.

At another university, an attractive coed is pretending to be a rigid racial bigot as part of an experiment testing how groups react to this type of deviance. At a nearby clinic, a family and their son, who is a mental patient, are working together on a series of tasks devised by psychiatrists interested in assessing the role structure of the family and the son's position in it. At another stop, first-born children are being compared with later-born children in their susceptibility to pressures to conform to group norms. At the final stop we find a large team

[28] Elvin V. Semrad and John Arsenian, "The Use of Group Processes in Teaching Group Dynamics," *American Journal of Psychiatry* (1951), C: 358–363.

[29] On training groups, see Leland P. Bradford, J. R. Gibb, and Kenneth D. Benne (eds.), *T-Group Theory and Laboratory Methods* (New York: Wiley, 1964); Edgar H. Schein and Warren G. Bennis, *Personal and Organizational Change Through Group Methods; The Laboratory Approach* (New York: Wiley, 1965).

7

of researchers perfecting a technique for feeding every statement in a group discussion into a high-speed computer which reproduces almost instantaneous summaries of what is being said in a group. What gives these varied activities coherence is the recent rediscovery of small human groups, and a growing realization that we can materially advance our knowledge about them.

In its brief history, the study of small groups has made several important advances. First, the trichotomy between the individual, the group, and society is gradually being resolved. Rather than conceiving of the person as *outside* the group, largely pitted against and contending with it, he is more frequently seen as being *in* the group and *of* society. A case in point is soldiers in battle who are simultaneously being themselves, being a group, and identifying with their nation when they fight for and seek security in each other. The affinity between person and group is becoming more apparent. This is partly because data-collecting techniques are extending beyond elements which are not shared (such as overt behavior) to include elements which are sharable (such as feelings, ideas, beliefs, values). Extension to sharable elements provides new information about those processes that are both personal and collective.

A second advance is the shift of emphasis from study of the group's effect on either its members or its environment to analysis of the group itself, from its influence to its process, from its output to its internal dynamics. Operationally, this has meant a shift from depending exclusively upon measures taken *before* and *after* group operation, to recording and analyzing processes *during* the group's operation. This advance goes hand-in-hand with the development of adequate methods for tracing group processes.

The third advance is the successful application of the experimental method. Rather than taking groups as they happen to exist, researchers have created them according to their own purposes, introduced experimental variations, and effectively tested hypotheses.

A fourth advance, as indicated above, is the invention of the self-analytic group. Instead of having the observer outside the group, groups have been composed of persons who simultaneously act as participants and observers, who interact and exchange their observations and interpretations. New information is being gained on what is relevant and important to group members.

Finally, as noted in the cases of Parsons and Bales and in the development of mathematical models, an advance is being made in the application of general system theory.

Though the sociology of small groups is too new a discipline for anyone to say where it will lead, some of its frontiers are apparent. It needs to devise methods for tracing latent group processes such as feelings, wishes, and unconscious assumptions; it needs to examine the transformations of long-term groups from their origin to their dissolution; it needs to expand to widely different cultures and to test how culture affects group process; it needs to know how studying and experimenting on groups alters them; and most of all it needs to create new theories to apply to group phenomena even after the groups themselves have become aware of the theories.

Aims of This Book

The first of four aims of this book is to introduce the sociological way of thinking about groups. Six major working models are presented and evaluated in Chapter One; they range from the older mechanical and organismic models to the more recent, and still tentative, cybernetic model.

The second aim is to acquaint the reader with the social context in which

introduction

the investigator gathers his basic information about groups. In Chapters Two and Three, the reader is invited into the laboratory, where he can put himself into the place of the scientific observer. There he not only can appreciate the difficulties the scientist, as an outsider, has in obtaining inside group information, but also can come to understand how the difficulties are overcome and how a science of groups is possible. Observational methods are described in Chapter Two, and the experimental method is discussed in Chapter Three.

The third aim is to introduce the five levels on which group processes occur: behavior, feelings, norms, goals, and values, and to relate those levels to the subjective experience of group members. As the levels are presented in Chapters Four and Five, the reader is invited to put himself in the place of a newcomer to the group and to follow his experience as he progresses from one level to another—or, more specifically, as he advances from a novice who has yet to learn what the group is, to one who eventually assumes executive responsibility for the group as a whole, and consequently requires a way of conceiving of it.

The final aim is to introduce the view that the group, as a whole, is a dynamic system with potential for change and growth. Although sociologists agree on this general point, there is lack of agreement on its implications. Without attempting to take all points of view into account, Chapter Six presents a paradigm which is based both on the cybernetic model (described in Chapter One) and upon the idea that group growth is not gradual but occurs instead as relatively sudden transformations from one type of system to another. Such transformations depend directly upon whether group members have adequately resolved certain critical organizational and emotional issues. Chapter Eight discusses in more detail two of these—authority and intimacy—showing the effects of their resolution upon the group's potential for growth.

In short, the book's emphasis is upon ways of thinking about groups, rather than upon a review of current research findings. The first reason back of this choice is that the empirical findings in a field that is both young and rapidly expanding are too numerous and varied to be easily consolidated and briefly reported. The second reason is that research operations on groups are not yet standardized. Consequently, the results which are the outcome of particular procedures and a particular setting need, in each case, to be interpreted and evaluated with full knowledge of these particulars. This is best done by referring to the original research reports themselves. It is hoped that, with the present book as an introduction, past and future accounts of research will gain fuller meaning and that the reader will have an added sense of excitement as he follows the venture of making a science of the sociology of small groups.

models
of groups

one

It should come as no surprise that group members and sociologists alike have their own mental models of groups: through past experience we all accumulate impressions and compose images of what groups are and how they operate. We "know" how boys play, what girls talk about, what families are like, how committees work. We "know" what is likely to happen in that lifeboat at sea, for we carry primitive notions, or working models, about "group nature" just as we do about "human nature." And even if vague, such images will affect orientations to a group, and collectively influence its history, for they are frames within which members tend to think and act. When events fall within the frame they seem natural and normal, but when they fall outside they are strange, if not inconceivable. Our images set limits both on what we think will happen and on what we imagine to be possible. For example, committees whose members "know" that committees don't work rarely work well, and groups whose members "know" that leaders make the decisions anyway rarely decide matters democratically. In this sense, groups tend in their actions to fulfill the prophecy contained in their models.

In its broadest sense the sociology of small groups is a self-conscious attempt to create workable models of groups—workable in the sense that they help organize disparate data into a more coherent whole, that they are stated clearly enough to be understood by others, that they seem to be consonant with our intersubjective experience of reality, and that their implications can be examined and tested and modified in terms of alternative ones. Like the group member, the sociologist builds his model out of experience and knowledge; and, like the member, his model affects his orientation to groups: it provides a frame for defining what is relevant or irrelevant, what is observable and what is not, what is comprehensible and what is not, what is testable and what is not, and so on. To a large extent the model governs his strategy of study and research. Often he is subject to pressures causing him to ignore realities (which, though important, are irrelevant to his model) and to search for groups which, because of their peculiar properties, fulfill the prophecy contained in his model. Yet, because his attempt is both self-conscious and in collaboration with fellow sociologists, he is subject to other pressures both to formulate his ideas clearly so they may be evaluated by others, and to subject them continually to reexamination and test. Certainly his model is useful when it contributes to sociology, yet it is no less useful when it helps members understand their group milieu.

Unfortunately for the student, there is no single model accepted at present by most sociologists as *the* working one. The state of small-group theory is, as we have said, neither that neat nor settled, but instead is in flux. This is partly because if small-group researchers have discovered anything over the past 30 or so years, it is that human groups are more complex, more varied, and perhaps more interesting than they first appear to be. One reaction has been to build more refined models of more highly selected facets, as illustrated by mathematical formulations,[1] while another has been to shift from closed to open models, from simplistic to more complex, from static to more dynamic, and from those that assume a few types of groups to those that acknowledge a wide variety.[2] Our discussion in this chapter emphasizes the second trend because it gives a broader and less technical introduction.

Before presenting a selection of models we should note first that although not all of them (the organismic, for example) were originally designed for small groups, they may nonetheless be applied to groups; and second that since few working models are presented explicitly in the literature, but must be reconstructed from implicit notions underlying approaches to groups, our sketches of models are interpretive. They are interpretations of implicit ideas employed in different approaches to the study of groups.

The Quasi-Mechanical Model

The group is like a machine—an interaction machine.[3] In response to universal personal needs, universal conditions of communication, and standard requirements of the problem-solving process, the group generates a series of actions, each of which can be classified according to its main function. One act with its function stimulates (with a certain probability) another act with its function, which in turn is the stimulus for a subsequent act, and so on. A question, for example, stimulates an answer which calls forth an evaluative response (positive or negative). Since acts are classified as functions they are essentially unchanging elements (one occurring early in group life is equal to one occurring later on) which may be added up and otherwise arithmetically manipulated to represent how the group operates.

[1] Herbert A. Simon, *Models of Man: Social and Rational* (New York: Wiley, 1957).
[2] For a variety of current approaches, see A. Paul Hare, Edgar F. Borgatta, and Robert F. Bales (eds.), *Small Groups; Studies in Social Interaction* (New York: Knopf, 1955), pp. 54–187.
[3] For a critique of this and other models see Karl W. Deutsch, *The Nerves of Government* (New York: The Free Press of Glencoe, 1963), pp. 22–50.

11

According to the mechanical model, group interaction follows universal and unchanging laws. Group behavior is like a game that is played over and over again so many times that one knows both the game and the players well enough to predict what will happen next. The general laws apply to such features as *who* will tend to speak, to *whom* they will speak, trends in types of behavior from the beginning to the end of the meeting, and so on. Bales, in particular, has sought to discover these laws and to construct coherent models from them.[4] His models emphasize the importance of the problem-solving situation. Although they acknowledge that some role is played by other factors, such as the larger society to which the group belongs, the group's own purpose, the variety of personalities in its membership and the type of problem being faced, that role is minor compared to the intellectual problems and the emotional forces that are brought into play when a number of individuals face a problem that must be solved. From this viewpoint the immutable core of the small group is the lawfulness of interaction when persons confront a problem together.

The model assumes that acts and members can be substituted for without fundamentally altering the system. An act that (let us say) functions to release tension is replaceable by a different one that does the same, and a group part (for instance, a child's mother) may be replaced by a different but similar-acting part (in this case a stepmother), in both cases without basically altering the group. (The model of course excludes the feelings of child and stepmother, except insofar as they affect overt action.) This assumption of replaceability also extends to norms and other elements of culture. One may replace the group's rules with another set because the universal laws are expected to apply equally well over a wide range of normative systems and in spite of normative differences. The group may even replace its conception of itself with another (such as being aware that it is following laws of interaction) without undergoing basic changes.

The aim of the sociologist using this type of a model is to discover the invariant and universal systematics in groups. His procedure is to construct a tentative model, observe a sample of groups, check the fit between model and observation, and—where the fit is poor—alter the model so that it applies to the greatest number of cases. The researcher's interest is not in differences between groups but in similarities. His model is improved to the degree to which it states a set of universal principles according to which unchanging elements operate.

Such models as we are discussing are valuable because they assert that our interpersonal processes are far more ordered, far more systematic, than common sense or the doctrine of the uniqueness of the individual, the family, the club, the nation (and so on) would have us assume. Observed differences are often obvious (and comforting), while similarities are more subtle (and often offensive). Quasi-mechanical models, although they have led (and may well continue to lead) to discoveries of regularities that sociology needs to know and understand,[5] at the same time are subject to two major limitations: one of substance and one in application. First, except for laying down the criteria of regularity and lawfulness, these models contain no independent standard of what is relevant and important for sociology and group members. It is an elementary error to equate relevance with uniformity—as we are reminded by the study of language,

[4] Robert F. Bales, "The Equilibrium Problem in Small Groups," in Talcott Parsons, Robert F. Bales, and Edward A. Shils, *Working Papers in the Theory of Action* (New York: The Free Press of Glencoe, 1953), pp. 111–161.

[5] For one sample of empirical generalizations, see Bernard Berelson and Gary A. Steiner, *Human Behavior: An Inventory of Scientific Findings* (New York: Harcourt, Brace, 1964).

12

models of groups

wherein it is found that more often than not it is just those properties *least* important to its service as a medium of communication that seem to behave lawfully.[6] Second, in its application, a model of selected processes often stands for the total processes: as more and more data are collected on behalf of the model, relatively less and less knowledge is gained about the aspects that it excludes, with the result that excluded aspects tend to become vague and forgotten. Since mechanical models usually exclude group emotion, norms, beliefs, and values, they deemphasize the significance of their cumulative effects, and consequently are not well equipped to explain evolution and group growth.

The Organismic Model

The group is like an organism—a biological organism.[7] It forms, grows, and reaches a state of maturity. It begins with a set of constituent elements—individuals with certain personalities, certain needs, ideas, potentialities, limitations—and in the course of development evolves a particular pattern of behavior, a set of indigenous norms, a body of beliefs, a set of values, and so on. Parts become differentiated, each assuming special functions in relation to other parts and the whole; yet these parts are integrated by a complex set of connections, interchanges, and coordinating mechanisms. As a group approaches maturity it becomes even more complex, more differentiated, more interdependent, and more integrated.

Like an organism, the group's internal purpose is self-fulfillment (though usually undefined); and, like an organism, its orientation to the outside world is to assure self-preservation both by protecting itself from external dangers and by exploiting its environment for its own needs.

A group is a natural phenomenon in the sense that it has a natural course of development determined essentially by the set of constituent elements with which it is born. A group's history is the story of the unfolding of the potentials within these elements. Groups with similar original components (such as personalities of members, cultural background, needs, values) tend to have similar histories; groups with different components (girls versus boys, adolescents versus adults, Negroes versus whites, dull persons versus bright ones) will follow their distinctly different (though every bit as natural) unfolding processes.

The model views the group as a more complex system than do quasi-mechanical models. It provides for change and development and for a wide variety of internal factors affecting development; and from its viewpoint interdependence is more than mutual influence. For example, when the stepmother replaces the real mother, the total organism of the family is changed: it is a different being with different components and relations and is therefore expected to alter its natural course of development.

One side-effect upon investigators who think about groups in terms of the organismic model is a reluctance to actively interfere with established groups;

---

[6] Joseph H. Greenberg, "Language and Evolution," in Betty J. Meggers (ed.), *Evolution and Anthropology: A Centennial Appraisal* (The Anthropological Society of Washington, 1959), pp. 61–75.

[7] Although the origins of the organismic model are ancient, a distinctively sociological formulation is Herbert Spencer's *The Study of Society* (New York: Appleton, 1896–1897). For a discussion of the organismic conception, see Harry Elmer Barnes and Howard Becker, *Social Thought from Folklore to Science* (New York: Heath, 1938), pp. 664–692. Few modern scientists or practitioners accept an explicit organismic model, yet it remains an important part of the implicit working models of outstanding modern practitioners; for example, see Elvin Semrad, *et al.*, "The Field of Group Psychotherapy," *International Journal of Group Psychotherapy* (1963), XIII: 352–475.

and a side-effect upon group members is to be wary of outsiders who might interfere too much with them or experiment on them. Each group, to repeat, has its own *natural way*, its natural course of development according to a determinate yet unknown plan. The role of the member is of course to participate in the plan's unfolding. The role of the investigator is to discover and understand the plan —and this he must do by observing natural groups in natural settings: he studies families at home, students at school, groups on the street corner, committees in the conference room. He must study *real* groups, performing *real* functions in *real* circumstances. But since the intrusion of foreign elements alters the natural way, he must keep his distance so as not to interfere: penetration of the group's boundary would not only change the group but might damage it. The student of real processes in real groups, knowing this, somewhat mistakenly imagines himself unfree to observe directly, to tape-record, to interview before the group is ended—in fact, to in any way "break the skin" of the group. (And he is definitely not free to set up groups on his own, to compare them at will, or to experiment with them, since to take the initiative would be to presume the role of creator—to play as it were the role of God, for his own ends.) The organismic conception of groups thus can be seen to support a conservative, passive, non-interfering role for the investigator—a role often reinforced by group members when (as we shall see in Chapter Two) they fear that their group will be fundamentally altered if observed, recorded, or such. Whether held by investigator or by subject, the doctrine of noninterference is associated with the assumption that the group, like an organism, must indeed "keep its skin unbroken" if it is to remain undamaged and to pursue its natural course. And so the investigator who employs the organismic model tends to forego vigorous means of entering into or experimenting with groups.

The Conflict Model

According to this model the group is like an arena in that it is a place where one sees an endless series of conflicts.[8] Group experience *is* conflict. It is a response to the reality that there is a shortage of what people need and want. One of the conditions of life is that no group has sufficient resources to fulfill all internal needs and to meet all external demands. In particular, there is a scarcity of *freedom, position,* and *resources*. To organize, a group must coordinate one part with another, and in doing so must limit the freedom of some parts. So long as persons value freedom, there is an inevitable conflict between their latitude, and demands upon them for conformity and coordination. Too, some members are more competent, more powerful, and more prestigeful than others; and, since the interests of those on top are opposed to those on the bottom, positional conflict also is unavoidable. And further, groups accept and reward some members more fully than others, and this inequality creates yet another type of conflict. (Even those groups that form because of their common opposition to something external experience these internal conflicts.)

[8] For the conflict model of groups, as in the case of other models, principles which were originally formulated for the larger society are either explicitly or implicitly applied to the small group. For a discussion of conflict theories of societies see Don Martindale, *The Nature and Types of Sociological Theory* (Boston: Houghton Mifflin, 1960), pp. 127–207. Also see Lewis Coser, *The Functions of Social Conflict* (New York: The Free Press of Glencoe, 1956); and Ralf Dahrendorf, *Class and Class Conflict in Industrial Society* (Stanford: Stanford University Press, 1959). For an application to small group structure, see Theodore A. Caplow, "A Theory of Coalitions in the Triad," *American Sociological Review* (1956), XXI: 489–493.

14

models of groups

Although the conflict model acknowledges the existence of integrative mechanisms, it confines their use to retrospective explanations of how the group held together, not to predictions of the future. Change, which occurs at every moment, is determined both in direction and in quality by the manner in which conflicts are resolved. Response to conflict determines the new state of the system. And though one conflict may be reduced, its résolution will be accompanied by new strains, so that the course of group history can be described by its endless sequential confrontation of conflict. No group is conflict-free; when one seems so, it is possible that it is in conflict over facing its real conflicts.

If it is generally true, as many clinical observations would suggest, that groups as well as individuals deny, cover over, and project onto others their internal conflicts, especially when they are uncertain about their ability to cope with them, then one value of this model is to focus attention on the conflicts, dissatisfactions, discomforts, and hostilities which may affect the group, but which members are either not aware of or are not free to manifest. The model's admonition to assume the existence of conflict until the contrary is proven circumvents both these defenses and the contagious beliefs of strong and satisfied members that everyone else in the group is satisfied. It counteracts, as well, the assumption of the organismic model that change is a natural unfolding process, rather than the result of contention over interests and desires.

Nonetheless, the model's emphasis results in limitations. First, it obscures the question of how and why groups do hold together; it overlooks the possibility of mutual respect in spite of hierarchical prestige ranking, of trust in spite of different interests, of the granting of freedom even at a cost to the self, of friendship and affection in spite of structural dissimilarities. In assuming scarcity, the model is unprepared to handle these groups or those sectors of groups which enjoy affluence. Second, it obscures the importance of the conflict-free area in group change. For instance, it is a simple and familiar fact that groups often shift direction either because they have attained their original goal or because they have realized its inadvisability, or because they have improved their techniques through learning, or because they have gained new knowledge about their situation. Such changes are accomplished not through conflict but through consensus. Finally, in applying the model there is the danger of assuming that *existing* conflicts are the most important phenomena for sociology and for the group member, or leader, to manage. One may imagine the leader who takes the conflict model as his only serious guide for action: *e.g.*, a mother frantically quelling one squabble after the other among her children, instead of getting on with the work of the day; or the manager of the firm who is distracted into keeping the peace instead of leading the company. By-and-large, both mothers and managers have a broader perspective on conflict—as do some of the following models.

The Equilibrium Model

The group is a system in equilibrium. Any disturbance, whether from inside or out, tends to be counteracted by opposing forces so that the system returns to the state prior to the disturbance. The clearest statement and application of this model to small groups has been made by Bales, who proposes that a push toward achieving the group goal disrupts solidarity and consequently tends to be followed by efforts to pull the group together again— and that, since this reconsolidation deflects energy from goal achievement, it tends to be followed by a renewed push toward the goal. And so it goes, until a point of equilibrium is reached between the pushing and pulling tendencies; or, more accurately, a moving point, because both the distance from the goal and the solidifying mechanisms may alter in the process.[9] Bales' model includes more group elements than both Festinger's theory of dissonance, which refers to cognition,[10] and Heider's balance theory, which includes affective and evaluative processes,[11] yet all three conceive of their respective processes as operating according to an equilibrium principle. A disturbance, dissonance, or imbalance creates strain or tension, which tends to be followed by an attempt, successful or not, to restore the system to a state of integration, consonance, or balance.

The value of the equilibrium model is that it simply and coherently organizes highly complex and interdependent phenomena. Yet, because of its simplicity, it must be applied with circumspection and restraint. Perhaps most important, one must specify the sector of the total system to which it is being applied, distinguishing it from sectors where it is not applicable.[12] To illustrate the point, let us take the experience of a young couple having a baby.

The wife becoming pregnant, the birth, the addition to the household— all these are changes which "disturb" the previous arrangement shared by a young married couple. If we were to apply the equilibrium model, with the discipline and naïveté required in using theoretical models, we would expect, on the basis of the model alone, responses to the arrival of the third party which would tend to return the system to its previous state. This would involve reducing the triad to a dyad—in other words, getting rid of the baby! Now, it is true that one often finds traces of such a tendency (such as fantasies of infanticide), but the emphatic tendency, of course, is not for the couple to act on such fantasies, but instead to transform themselves on the baby's behalf. The man becomes a father as well as a husband; the woman a mother as well as a wife; while together they become parents of a child. The parties respond to birth by fundamentally reconstituting their group.

Although application of the equilibrium model is nonsensical in this case because one "knows" it should not be used for *that* part of the system, misapplication is not easy to detect in less familiar settings. The problem is a general one, for while one may find a sector of a group that operates according to the model, one can usually find sectors that do not; and, while a group in its totality may follow the model for a brief period, since members die and most small groups dissolve it is unlikely that any group as an over-all system follows the model *ad infinitum*. Consequently, its users need to specify both the sector and the duration for which the model is thought to hold.

Another lesson in the illustration is the model's bias in viewing major events, particularly external influences, primarily as disturbances to be avoided or, failing that, as the causes of damage to be repaired. In doing so it overlooks those external influences which are perceived by insiders as good, helpful, and therefore welcome. The baby may symbolize these, but the list is long: news

[9] Robert F. Bales, "Adaptive and Integrative Changes as Sources of Strain in Social Systems," in Hare, Borgatta, and Bales (eds.), Small Groups, pp. 127–131; and Robert F. Bales, "The Equilibrium Problem in Small Groups," in Parsons, Bales, and Shils, Working Papers in the Theory of Action, pp. 111–161.
[10] Leon Festinger, A Theory of Cognitive Dissonance (Evanston: Row, Peterson, 1957).
[11] Fritz Heider, "Attitudes and Cognitive Organization," Journal of Psychology (January 1946), XXI: 107–112.
[12] For discussions of the limitations of the equilibrium model see David Easton, "The Limits of the Equilibrium Model in Social Research," Behavioral Science (April 1956), I: 96–104; and Theodore M. Mills, "Equilibrium and the Processes of Deviance and Control," American Sociological Review (1959), XXIV: 671–679.

16

about the outside world; visitors such as a neighbor, the doctor, or a friend; a new technique or a new art form; and so on. Groups respond to such welcome intrusions by increasing their receptivity so that they can benefit, rather than by reverting to some previous state. When one wants to predict direction of system-change in such cases, it is more important to know the positive or negative value placed upon the "disturbance" than to know the.nature of the system's previous state.

The Structural-Functional Model

The group is a goal-seeking, boundary-maintaining system whose survival is problematical. It is a mutable and transitory arrangement of actions, norms, ideas, and techniques devised (though seldom entirely consciously) to meet the demands of personal, social, and environmental realities. It is subject not only to constant change, but to a cessation of functions or even disintegration unless real demands are adequately met. At each moment the group (through its agents) must exercise intelligence and ingenuity, mobilize its resources, and act positively in meeting changing demands. Parsons, Bales, and Shils separate demands, and capabilities for meeting them, into four areas: [13]

(1) *Adapatation*—when external resources are cut off, the group must be able to find new ones; when current techniques become obsolete or ineffective, it must invent new ones.

(2) *Goal attainment*—when blocks appear before the goal, it must be able to circumvent them; when members become confused or frustrated or distracted, it must be able to reorient them and remobilize their resources.

(3) *Integration*—when one part of the group threatens to destroy other parts, the group must be able to check, protect, and coordinate them; it must bridge differences between the strong and the weak, the competent and the inept, the active and the passive, and so on; it must create concepts or symbols of itself as a collective unit that unites its sub-parts.

(4) *Pattern-maintenance*—in the face of contrary pressures, the group must be able to sustain its standard procedures, reinforce members' feelings and affective relations, enforce its rules, confirm its beliefs and affirm its values; and it must, for example, be able to "remember" its customs from one meeting to the next.

The model assumes that members will be gratified as the group progresses toward its goal. Moreover, it assumes that some group members (or some part of each of them) will serve as group agents whose purpose is to assure the group's survival so that it may continue to gratify members through pursuit of its goal. The functions of agents are, at each moment: (1) to observe what is happening; (2) to assess the effects of events upon goal-attainment and survival; and (3) according to this assessment, to take action. To "take action" means to *redirect* a process when it is likely to miss the group goal; to *reinforce* it when it is headed toward the goal; and, simultaneously, to *counteract* any negative effects that goal effort might have upon adaptation, integration, and pattern-maintenance, but to *support* them when their effects are positive. In addition, the agents' function is to learn from this experience and to infuse this learning into the group's culture. In short, in response to the four sets of de-

[13] Parsons, Bales, and Shils, *Working Papers in the Theory of Action*, pp. 63–109; 179–190.

mands, group agents act and learn on behalf of the group—learning how to achieve the collective goal, and how to assure the group's survival.

Depending upon the skill of its agents, a group tends toward a balance, or an oscillating sequence, between the multiple demands of adaptation, goal-attainment, integration, and pattern-maintenance. Change is determined by the interplay of these demands, the accumulated learning in how to meet them, and the effective use of that learning. The model acknowledges the fact that many groups fail to achieve their goals and that some groups do not even survive. Achievement and survival depend upon the adequacy of techniques and learning relative to actual existing demands, so that determining their likelihood in the case of any specific group requires empirical investigation.

The model makes several important contributions to the sociology of small groups. First, it acknowledges the role of learning and, consequently, the role of culture and its accumulation. Group culture evolves through the assessment and reassessment of how the group meets demands. And while the model acknowledges the fact that many groups replace ineffective ways with more effective ones, it escapes the assumption that progress, or positive evolution, is an inevitable process. Its second contribution is to connect motivation of the individual member to group survival. The group must gratify its members; it must attract and sustain their interest; it must fulfill, or hold a promise of fulfilling, certain of their needs. Promise of gratification ties the individual to the group, and the members' investment in the group provides it with motivational energy. This is an important contrast to the mechanical model, which implicitly assumes the source of energy to be outside the system, and to the organismic model, which assumes an internal but unspecified source.

Contrary to the views of critics of structural-functional analysis,[14] the model does afford systematic treatment of group disintegration: when requirements for survival are correctly identified but groups do not fulfill them, then groups disintegrate. Confusion on this question arises through misuse of the model. When, in the name of structural-functional analysis, the sociologist assumes that all observable events and structural arrangements have, because of their existence, a positive effect upon survival and goal-attainment, he is misusing the model. For the model requires that before the investigator draws conclusions about the functional significance of group properties, he must determine independently what is and what is not a positive function.

Another criticism is more justified—namely, that the model has a conservative bias. Not that it favors the *status quo* (holding a group together so that it can learn more effectively how to pursue its goal does not suggest a stationary group), but that *survival* is a conservative criterion. Groups may survive while exacting a high price of pain, confusion, and frustration from their members; they may survive while operating at a fraction of their potential. While helpful in establishing basic requirements, the standard of survival is simply not enough when one is dealing with groups capable of far more than maintaining themselves—capable of growth and advancement. As we shall see, the next model shifts emphasis from survival to growth, from simply meeting existing demands to increasing capabilities for meeting a wide range of possible demands, and from pursuing a given goal to developing abilities for achieving a variety of goals. Compared to such a model, the structural-functional dependence upon the criterion of survival is conservative.

---

[14] Ralf Dahrendorf, "Out of Utopia: Toward a Reorientation of Sociological Analysis," *American Journal of Sociology* (September 1958), LXIV: 115–127; also David Lockwood, "Some Remarks on 'The Social System,' " *British Journal of Sociology* (June 1956), VII: 134–146.

18

models of groups

The Cybernetic-Growth Model

Human groups are information-processing systems potentially capable of increasing their capabilities. Like the structural-functional model of Parsons, Bales, and Shils, the cybernetic model of Deutsch assumes the existence of group agents who observe, assess the situation, and act with consequence upon the situation they observe.[15] When, in the face of either internal or external demands these operations are unsatisfactory or inadequate, the group suffers impairment at the least, and in the extreme, destruction. On the other hand, when conditions are favorable and the operations are effective, the group not only survives but becomes capable of monitoring itself, altering its direction, determining its own history and learning how to learn to determine its history—with the consequence that it accumulates and expands its capabilities, or *grows*.

Self-determination and growth depend upon three orders of feedback of increasing complexity and importance. The first is goal-seeking feedback, which is assumed in the structural-functional model and exemplified in Deutsch's terms by the homing torpedo. With a collective goal in mind, group agents determine by observation whether current actions are taking the group toward or away from the target. When the reading is positive, the agents may do nothing. When it is negative, they attempt to decrease the error by altering the way the group acts on the environment—whereupon they read the effects of their intervention and, if necessary, again redirect operations in the environment in order to minimize the error. Through observation, intervention, and observation of the effects of intervention, then, group agents *learn* how to operate on the environment to achieve collective goals.

The second order of feedback is more complex, for it involves a rearrangement, or a reconstitution, of the group itself. Let us speak for the moment as though feedback processes were all at the conscious level. When agents observe a basic incongruence or incompatibility between the habits, customs, beliefs, techniques, and so on, of the group and external realities, one step is to consider how rearrangement of the group might improve the fit; a second is to attempt to alter the internal components of the group; a third is to assess the effects of these attempts; while the final one is to learn from a series of attempts effective ways of accomplishing internal rearrangements. We can return to the example of the birth of a baby to illustrate incongruity and internal rearrangement. Were the relation between husband and wife to remain unchanged upon the arrival of a baby, that relationship would be incongruent with reality. But as they acquire the new roles of father and mother, and of joint parent—as they learn to become parents—their arrangement more nearly fits reality. Their reconstitution as parents is what is meant by *second order feedback*. (Further examples are the constant alterations of their conceptions of the child as he matures, their ways of responding to him, their ways of teaching him, and so on.)

The third type of feedback is *consciousness*. Consciousness is a system's awareness of itself. A person contributes to his consciousness when in addition to acting he observes and formulates ideas about himself as an actor. A group contributes to its consciousness when in addition to responding to demands, its members formulate and communicate ideas about its character as a demand-meeting system. Consciousness is gained through adding to the function of acting the functions of observing and comprehending the system that is acting.

15 Deutsch, *The Nerves of Government*, pp. 75–142.

Let us use the analogy of the prism to clarify what is involved in comprehending the system. In looking at a lighted lamp from across a room, the average person concludes that there is nothing but air and some amount of "plain old lamplight" between the lamp and his eyes. However, when a prism is placed between lamp and eye, what was mere illumination of one color or another proves to be a highly differentiated spectrum—one which can provide information about even such esoteric matters as the nature of the source of that light. (Of course it takes special training to enable one to interpret such information, and at least a modicum of knowledge just to make him aware that it is of any consequence.) In an analogous way, when someone acts in a social setting, that act, being caused by the interplay of forces within the actor, among group members, and between the group and the external world, contains sets of information about the total situation and about its various causes. The trained observer (whether member or outsider), using (as it were) his mind's eye as his prism, sees these sets, or types of messages, to be meaningful, and is able to unscramble, decode, and arrange them.

Although a more refined breakdown is presented in Chapter Six, two very general sets of such information are: (1) those that indicate an act's relation to demands placed upon the system; and (2) those that indicate the nature of, or changes in the nature of, the system itself. For example, a member suggesting a successful solution to a problem is in the first set, while the fact that he alone among others had been silent until making the suggestion is in the second set; a team's making a touchdown is in the first set, while the fact that the play was not according to plan is in the second set. When members decode messages which contain information about the group, formulate ideas about what the group is and what it is doing, and convey these ideas to others, then those members are operating as agents of group consciousness. They read and feed back into the group information about its processes and structure.

All three orders of feedback are necessary for self-determination. They are used in combination, for example, by the quarterback responsible for his team's play. He reads the weaknesses in the other team's defenses and tries to capitalize on them (goal-seeking); due to unforeseen circumstances, he may have to revise the pre-game strategy, trying out one modification after the other (internal rearrangement); and on each play he assesses the developing weaknesses or strengths in his team, and, in general, the present state and condition of his team (consciousness). Since he can act on his ideas—observe the effects of his action and therefore test them—he is in a position to learn how to learn to direct his team. Through self-monitoring, self-steering, and testing these processes, he is able to increase his capabilities for self-determination.

In the light of this explanation, it is not hard to see that (or why) processes which enable self-determination affect group growth. Self-monitoring shows both what the group is and what it is not, which resources are utilized and which are not, what its goals are and what they are not. Self-steering, and monitoring the steering operation, show where the group is going, its flexibility in changing directions, and, by implication, where else it might go. By what it shows, consciousness introduces knowledge about unrealized potential, and notions about alternative goals. Consciousness expands any group's conception of its possibilities. By feeding these ideas back for test, and by acting upon the appropriate ones, the group gains a capacity for growth.

But what, more specifically, is meant by growth? Not an increase in membership, but an increase in capabilities for meeting a wider range of possible demands. Using the structural-functional classification of demand areas, we suggest the following set of indicators of group growth:

20

Indications of a Small Group's Capacity to Grow

1. *Adaptation*
   a. ". . . an increase in openness—that is, an increase in the range, diversity, and effectiveness of [a group's] *channels of intake* of information from the outside world. . . ." [16]
   b. Capacity to extend the scope of the group's contacts and obligations beyond current boundaries
   c. Capacity to alter the group's customs, rules, techniques, and so on, to accommodate new information and new contracts
2. *Goal-attainment*
   a. Capacity to hold goal-seeking effort in abeyance while alternative goals are being considered
   b. Capacity to shift to, or add, new goals
3. *Integration*
   a. Capacity to differentiate into sub-parts while maintaining collective unity
   b. Capacity to export resources without becoming impoverished and to send emissaries without losing their loyalty
4. *Pattern-maintenance and extension*
   a. Capacity to receive new members and to transmit to them the group's culture and capabilities
   b. Capacity to formulate in permanent form the group's experience and learning and to convey them to other groups and to posterity

These few indicators are perhaps enough to suggest the important advance of the growth model over the survival model. Groups oriented toward survival attempt to maintain their boundaries while obtaining gratification, while growing groups penetrate and extend their boundaries. Growing groups are increasingly receptive to new signals, new possibilities, new responsibilities; they are increasingly confident both in admitting strangers and in spawning new groups; and they cross the boundaries of space and time by putting their experience in communicable form for others. From the viewpoint of the cybernetic-growth model of Deutsch, small groups are a *source* of experience, learning, and capabilities, rather than just *recipients*.

Group growth does not occur automatically but depends directly upon members who are both capable of personal growth, and committed to group development. Since each individual is himself an information-processing system, the model can be applied to him as well as to the group as a whole. He may employ the three orders of feedback: process information from his external world, from his past, and from his present state; develop ability to monitor and to govern himself; and acquire the ability to grow. In fact, unless he, or some other member is committed to group development, no advance in the group's capabilities can be expected. This is to say that all information processes we have attributed to the group are actually performed by and through individuals as essential components of the collective system. Whether viewed from the personal or the collective perspective, the capabilities of the persons as sub-parts place a ceiling upon the capabilities of the collectivity. It is to say that the application of the cybernetic-growth model to small groups presumes its simultaneous application to individual members. In this sense then it is a model of both personal and group growth. Though space is not available for a detailed application, the following outline suggests indicators of personal growth.

[16] *Ibid.*, p. 140.

Indicators of a Person's Capacity to Grow

1. *Adaptation*
   a. Receptivity to a wider range of information about himself, others, his groups, his and other societies, and the physical environment
   b. Receptivity to new freedoms, responsibilities, and obligations—to new roles
   c. Flexibility in modifying his ideas, beliefs, personal norms, and emotional attachments without loss of intellectual or moral integrity
2. *Goal-attainment*
   a. Capacity to postpone immediate gratification, and to conceive of and evaluate an increasing number of avenues for gratification
   b. Capacity to decommit himself from one goal, and to recommit himself to new and additional goals, and to learn how to attain them
3. *Integration*
   a. Capacity to perform in an expanded repertoire of roles and variety of social relations without suffering diffusion of his identity
4. *Pattern-maintenance and extension*
   a. Capacity for deeper emotional involvement with others without surrendering his self
   b. Increasing ability to convey his experience, learning, and capabilities to others

The cybernetic model is not complete unto itself as a small group's model. It refers to some, but not all, sectors of human systems. It refers to the information processing sector—but not to the sector of human drives, nor to the directions drives tend to take. One must go *outside* the model to understand what motivates the system—what pushes, pulls, or drives it; one must go outside to discover channels of *feelings*, their network, and the emotions that flow through them; and one must go outside to define the way biological and sociological realities structure the demands that must be met, and set limits upon system change (e.g., physical and emotional needs of the infant; personality structure and types of members; the structure of sex, age, and kinship relations). Note, for example, in the specification of personal and group growth that it was necessary to call upon the structural-functional model both for a classification of demands and for a bridge between personal motivation and information processing. This is just one indication that for a more complete model of small groups, sociology needs a composite of several models: Deutsch's cybernetic-growth model; the structural-functional model of Parsons, Bales, and Shils; and a model of emotional processes dimly suggested by Freud and more recently of interest to Bion, Redl, and others.[17] As a step toward the development of a composite model, the final chapter of this book presents a variety of types of emotional relations among members which differ in their capacity to generate new capabilities.

Among the cybernetic model's contributions, two stand out. First, it directs the outside observer's attention to the concrete moment of action, and to the information that is contained in and relevant to that moment—the present state of the system, its past, the relation of the system to its environment, and so on. This is an important step in a theoretical model because it is precisely the realities of the concrete moment of action that confront the member of the group and that must be managed by him. And what is relevant information for

---

[17] Sigmund Freud, *Group Psychology and the Analysis of the Ego* (New York: Liverwright, 1949); Bion, *Experiences in Groups*; Fritzl Redl, "Group Emotion and Leadership," *Psychiatry* (1942), V: 573–596, reprinted in abridged form in Hare, Borgatta, and Bales (eds.), *Small Groups*, pp. 71–87.

models of groups

the insider is precisely the information that is useful to the outside observer. Consciousness on the part of insiders (ideas about the nature of the system) corresponds to the substantive and professional aim of the outside observer (a sociological comprehension of the nature of the system). What the member learns about his group is relevant to the sociologist, and vice-versa. Under advantageous circumstances, advances in consciousness increase the capabilities of both. This is to say that the model assumes an inherent collaborative relation between group member and observer and, perhaps, anticipates a convergence of their viewpoints. (Yet, note that though viewpoints converge, responsibilities need not, for while the member's feedback responses alter the group, the sociologist's feedback responses alter his sociology.)

The model's second contribution is its provision for growth. Not only does it accord with the easily observable facts that both persons and groups learn and grow, as mentioned above, but it becomes a useful analytical tool when the sociologist encounters persons and groups who are interested in more than survival and immediate gratification; whose vision for the group includes new ideas, techniques, and goals; who are willing to assume responsibility for maximizing the general capabilities of the group; and who experience gratification when the group progresses toward that end. With a flexible growth-model the sociologist can keep in step with processes in the group; without one his sociology becomes dissassociated from groups that advance in capabilities.

Two Sources of Resistance in Studying Groups

The models summarized in this chapter are relatively simple, abstract formulations of selected dynamic processes in groups. They help organize and guide the sociologist's thinking. To perform that function throughout changes in knowledge and circumstance they must be on the one hand tentative and modifiable, and on the other constantly examined, tested, and, when necessary, modified according to observations of actual groups. For a lively and growing science there needs to be active interchange between model and findings, and sufficient flexibility both for new models and for new sources of data. Although such interchange is familiar in many sciences, it deserves attention in our discussion because of the special forms of resistance that arise when the human investigator studies human groups. Before adequate readings can be obtained, at least two major sources of resistance must be overcome; the first is in the groups being studied, and the second is experienced by the sociologist.

It is a familiar fact that when confronted with a stranger whose task is to scrutinize them, groups tend to close ranks and "clam up." To many persons such reaction affirms the belief that it is impossible to take authentic readings of real groups, and further supports the conclusion that the scientific study of groups is not feasible. To the sociologist, however, a group's defensive reaction (to him) is a fact of group life, a phenomenon that, first, he must understand and then (and if appropriate) he must alter, chiefly through developing a type of social relation with the group in which collective defense against him is no longer necessary. In the next two chapters (on Observation and Experimentation, respectively), more is said about group resistance and what the investigator can do about it. The methodological question of how to manage resistance is raised in this introductory book (and early in our discussion) not because readers are expected to become sociologists and face the issue in the same way sociologists do, but rather because skepticism, where it exists, is likely to persist until it is realized that with human groups, at least, it is entirely possible (though ad-

23

mittedly not the prevailing practice) to create a relationship where members not only feel comfortable in the presence of an investigator, but voluntarily cooperate with him and learn from him.

The second source of resistance is in the mind of the sociologist. Along with other social beings, he belongs to some groups but not to all those he knows about. While with his friends and associates, he feels *within* the group; while near a group to which he does not belong, he feels *outside* the group. The change in his feelings and thought as he moves from insider to outsider reinforces the belief that group boundaries are such that at any one time and place one is either on one or the other side of them—either inside or outside. Although many persons share such a belief, it is especially important to the sociologist, for it conflicts with what he is called on to do professionally; namely, to study in a detached manner persons close to him, and to gain rapport with strange persons in alien cultures.

The conflict is shown in the characteristic split of students of groups into two sets: the "clinical" and the "abstract-theoretical." The clinicians find it easy to identify personally with group members, yet hard to conceive of the group as a collectivity. The second set, the abstract-theoreticians, find it easy to intellectualize the group as a system, but hard to empathize with its members. One set perceives the group from within; the other, from without. The question of how one, whether he be investigator or group member, orients toward the group boundary is another issue raised in the next two chapters. It is suggested that boundaries, as products of the mind and the emotions, are rarely impenetrable. Just as in social intercourse they may be crossed, one's intellectual orientation may shift rapidly back and forth between an internal view and an external view; and, just as one person may at any one time belong to and be influenced by a number of groups, one's intellectual orientation may transcend the boundary separating inside from outside. One of the conditions that diminishes the sociologist's resistance and promises a systematic yet comprehensively human sociology of groups is man's capacity to "become stranger to the familiar" and to empathize with his alien counterpart.

In short, the sociologist must both create a workable relation with his groups, and acquire an intellectual viewpoint that transcends group boundaries, and in this respect, *make* his science possible. Of course, until one sees why he has to do this and how he does it, one is unlikely to become convinced that a science of groups is, in fact, possible—and so the why and how of this matter will be the subject of our next discussion.

models of groups

observation

two

For the essentials in building a science, the eminent physiologist L. J. Henderson suggested three ingredients: first, intimate contact and an habitual, intuitive familiarity with the phenomena; second, means for systematically collecting and ordering data; and, third, an effective way of thinking about the phenomena.[1] The relevance of his proposal for widely separated fields is apparent when, for example, we compare the astronomer and the sociologist of groups.

In the first place, through search, scanning, and repeated observation, the astronomer soon acquires a "feel" for the heavens, and a cognitive map of its particulars: objects, dimensions, relations, movements, and so on. Although at any one time he may not be able to reproduce all of its particulars, his map is of enormous service in locating where he is, in allowing him to concentrate in a selected area without losing touch with other areas, and, of course, in helping him to sense immediately any new and strange object. A comparable "feel" and "map" is acquired by the sociologist through direct and repeated contact with groups, through observation of a wide variety of groups, and through active participation in them. In time, and as figure and ground separate, he becomes sensitive to what is and is not happening in a group, to what the group is for-

---

[1] Lawrence J. Henderson, "Procedure in a Science," in Hugh Cabot and Joseph A. Kahl, *Human Relations, Concepts and Cases in Concrete Social Science*, Vol. I (Cambridge: Harvard University Press, 1953), pp. 24–39.

getting or avoiding, to shifts in rules, to changes in direction, and to conflicts before they become otherwise apparent.

Second, both astronomer and sociologist make systematic observations. While the astronomer takes readings on mass, density, rotation, speed, and direction of movement, the sociologist observes and records indicators of what group members do, say, feel, and think. Both use such readings as workable facts.

Third, both attempt to construct conceptions of their phenomena—abstract, simplified models, or theories,· which account for, or help to explain, a proportion of the facts. The heliocentric theory of the solar system is an example for astronomy; the boundary-maintaining system tending toward a state of equilibrium (referred to in Chapter One) is one from sociology.

In short, although astronomy and sociology are clearly different in subject matter, refinement of techniques, and theoretical sophistication, they are comparable in the types of procedures by which they make science out of their respective inquiries. Both require intuitive familiarity with the phenomena, systematic data, and an effective way of thinking about the phenomena.

Notwithstanding these similarities, however, an important procedural difference remains. Since sociology is man studying man, it is highly reflexive. As a human being, the sociologist cannot exclude himself from his inquiry, nor can he practically exclude how the men he studies influence him, nor how his study of man affects man. He can, of course, but to do so is, as Cooley suggested,[2] to discard one of his strongest assets—namely, his affinity with his object of study, his capacity to empathize with him, his opportunity to talk with and to learn from him. Because of this affinity and because of the reflexivity of sociology, we are obliged to add to Henderson's list a fourth ingredient: a collaborative exchange between the investigator and the investigated. As we know, even the most rudimentary description of a group requires a reciprocal relation between sociologist and group; the sociologist must contact the group and the group must open at least part of itself to the investigator. Beyond that, the growth of the field requires a skillfully devised social relationship wherein groups permit the investigator to become not only familiar but increasingly familiar with their operations, where systematic data may be collected not only on obvious and public matters but over an increasingly wide and deep range of phenomena, and where the ideas in the minds both of group members and sociologist about how groups operate may be exchanged, applied, tested, and reformulated. Because other procedures are contingent upon this relationship, this chapter begins with a consideration of the dynamic relation between observer and group; and, because the long-range growth of the sociology of groups depends upon the quality of interchange between group and investigator, the chapter ends with a prospectus for an optimal relationship. In between, the questions of what is observed and how it is observed are discussed. Chapter Three introduces the special problems that arise from experimentation, and the rest of the book deals with the problem of developing an effective way of thinking about groups.

The Observer and the Group

Many scientists, as we know, use special instruments (the microscope and the telescope are common examples) to bring their phe-

[2] Charles H. Cooley, "The Roots of Social Knowledge," *American Journal of Sociology* (July 1926), XXXII: 59–65; reprinted in Cabot and Kahl, *Human Relations*, pp. 60–71.

observation

nomena closer to them. As the worlds these instruments open become familiar, the scientist senses additional realms, and often devises new instruments (such as the electron microscope and the radio telescope, to maintain the example) to reach these new realms. In such instances, technology and the investigator work together both to increase the intimacy of contact and to extend the realm of phenomena with which the investigator may familiarize himself.

Much the same may be said for the social scientist, whose concern with groups causes him to find ways to be brought into ever closer and broader contact with group processes. But the technology through which this is accomplished is of a special kind. Because group processes occur within and among persons, and because both persons and groups surround themselves with boundaries which regulate access to these processes, the barriers separating groups and their investigators are more social, emotional, attitudinal, and cultural than they are physical. Consequently, the barriers must be transcended by social, psychological, and cultural means. The special technology (and the first technical procedure) of the investigator of groups is to devise that quality of social relation between himself and groups which allows him to come into sustained and intimate contact with the group.

Since effective construction of such a relation depends upon a comprehension of the boundary that separates the group from him, and more generally upon an understanding of the dynamics between insiders and outsiders, and since comprehension of these dynamics comes best through actual contact with groups, let us imagine an apprentice beginning his career as a sociologist, and trace the highlights of his experience in confronting groups.

The Dynamics of Familiarity

The apprentice's training program may take him to any of a number of different settings: the wardroom of a ship, a nursery school, a group therapy session, a training seminar for senior military personnel, a family conference in the living room.[3] Wherever, one of his first discoveries is that he is in direct and immediate contact with unique, concrete, unrehearsed, and largely unpredictable human processes. Events are disorderly and often incoherent, appearing to him in raw form, unfiltered by anyone else's interpretation of their meaning. Although he may be confused by lack of order and pattern, he can sense the possibility for independent observation and analysis. His first discovery, then, is the opportunity to become intuitively familiar with the phenomena—Henderson's first requirement.

Soon, contrary to the expectations of the popular belief, the apprentice is surprised by the extent to which people under observation reveal themselves. He finds that they are not always on guard, and as a consequence inadvertently becomes privy to information that, in certain circumstances, could seriously affect their lives. A military officer's castigation of his commander could ruin his own career; a corporation executive's offhand admission of illegal tax procedures could lead to his imprisonment; wives' intimate talk in group therapy could estrange their husbands; a young psychiatrist's ineptness in a training group could destroy his patients' faith in him. And in the laboratory, even the most attractive young lady, preening before a mirror, could mar her reputation

---

[3] On the observer's relation to groups in the field see William F. Whyte, "Observational Fieldwork Methods," in Marie Jahoda, Morton Deutsch, and Stuart W. Cook (eds.), *Research Methods in Social Relations*, Vol. II, 1st ed. (New York: Dryden, 1951), pp. 493–511; and E. Rosenfeld, "The American Social Scientist in Israel: A Case Study in Role Conflict," *American Journal of Orthopsychiatry*, XXVIII: 563–571.

27

as well as the image of her beauty by carelessly or absentmindedly probing deeply into her nose with her little finger. The apprentice learns that to be sure, some guards are up, but many others are down.

This experience of discovering the unexpected, the apprentice finds, affects his personal composure. When he sees more than he expects to, and more than members intend to reveal, and when there are no limits on what he should see or on what he should do with what he sees, he feels uneasy and embarrassed, as though he were stepping out of bounds—as if he were some sort of transgressor. (Such doubts about the right to observe were reflected in the dream of one observer following his first day with a therapy group: dressed in a doctor's white coat, he was in a courtroom being tried as a Peeping Tom before a greatly oversized microphone, which as the dream progressed seemed to him in his state of confusion to represent the judge.) Seeing too much violates childhood taboos and associates oneself with the spy, the snooper, or the voyeur—or with lonely persons who are neither entirely inside or outside. And not only the right to observe, but one's motivation in observing, comes into doubt. One could even come to see himself as a pervert or a blackmailer and become further upset by the jokes about observation laboratories and about those who work in them—jokes that play on the voyeuristic potentials. Anxiety over precisely this matter causes some apprentices to leave the role of observer altogether. Others, of course, overcome such occupational hazards and become perceptive observers of human processes.

Apprentice sociologists who stay discover that group members attribute to them superhuman powers. In their imagination, the observer misses no signals and forgets nothing. He is an all-seeing, all-knowing judge, and frequently is thought to be in collusion with the authority figure in the group, and aligned with those who have jurisdiction over the group. Members often warn their fellows against the power of the observer, as in the following quotation of a military officer in which the ostensible reference to someone at a distant base turns out to be a comment on the observer who is present in the room: "The important thing to remember here is that Sherril is just a spy, no more. He can't do anything—can't produce anything solid. He's just going around getting the dope and sending it over his hot line up above. Everybody should realize that he can make or break anybody on the base. A snooper like that can tear an organization apart." Is not this officer's concern generally shared by those being observed? (What is being done with the information about me? Can it be used against me? How safe are we? Who has the observer under control? Until we know, we either close ranks against him, or fall apart.)

One interpretation of these disturbances is that observation confuses traditional notions about boundaries. Whereas the observer's sitting on the side and being excluded from group activity affirms the existence of a boundary, his access to inside information denies the boundary. Although he is an outsider, he wants inside information and wants it without becoming an insider. And, while privy to the group, he remains outside its jurisdiction. In all these ways, and more, his presence implies a privileged position, with the right to take away information without giving anything in return, and to be above the group while it is "subject" to him.

It is a curious fact that groups both define the observer as being above them, and feel he takes something away from them. The mechanism is somewhat as follows: if *he* is the observer, then we need not make observations of our own; if he is a superior observer, then we'd *better not* make our observations; if he is the judge—a superior judge—then we'd better not make our own deci-

observation

sions. They more or less delegate to the outsider their own responsibilities, perhaps in the hope that he will oblige by performing them—for to observe, judge, and predict what happens is indeed a difficult task. When, however (in keeping within the limits of propriety recognized by the well-trained observer), he does not accept these responsibilities, they not only resent him but in the meantime have allowed their own capabilities to atrophy. They have become more watchful but less observant, more critical but less evaluative, more controlled but less committed. They often attribute their loss of these powers to the presence of the outside observer. The maneuver is defensive for there is no technical reason why group and observer cannot make independent observations, judgments, and decisions.

The apprentice next discovers that the group wants to observe *him*—a discovery sometimes made when it is least expected. For instance, on one occasion, a training group in a laboratory stopped abruptly and announced that it would go no further until the several observers were brought out from behind the mirrors, identified, and "given the opportunity" of explaining their *real* purposes in being there. This was a first step in "getting to really know the observers." Group members want to contact the observer—to have him respond and reveal himself—partly, of course, to correct their vague and oversized image of him, and partly to find out about themselves and to detect the standards he uses in judging them, but also, we suggest, to bring him into the group and under its jurisdiction.

Should it surprise us that in the meantime the observer discovers within himself a desire to join the group? Increasingly he wants to express his feelings toward members—his warmth toward some, his coolness toward others, his admiration for some, his distaste for others. Increasingly he empathizes with the leader, wanting to prompt him or advise him or discuss with him the philosophy of leadership. Increasingly his emotional state follows the emotional swings of the group. In the extreme he may identify with the group to the extent that he comes under all the influences it is under—as, for example, in taking the same experimental drugs the group is taking.

Our purpose in relating and discussing these things is to suggest that the presence of the observer contradicts the traditional notion of the boundary separating insider from outsider: the observer, to repeat, is an outsider wanting inside information without becoming an insider. The group can solidify its boundary and seal itself off against him, or the boundary may be dissolved bilaterally, to be re-formed to include him within its jurisdiction and thus to make him a member of the group. Note, however, that in either case science loses, for in both instances the apprentice vacates the role of independent scientific observer.

This all suggests that the balance of forces tends to move the investigator out of his role of scientist. His technical problem is to counteract these forces. His solution, in general terms, is to help reconstitute the group boundaries so that they may be both maintained and transcended: *maintained* through mutual respect for the legitimate and distinct purposes, first of group development, and second of scientific observation; and *transcended* through mutual appreciation of the essential kinship between the observer and the observed arising from their affinity as members of the human community. *How* this is to be accomplished will vary from one circumstance to another, but note that a solution is *critically important* to the sociology of groups. On the one hand, if the boundaries are not transcended, the group will repel the investigator, and if they are not maintained it will incorporate him; on the other hand, if they are both tran-

29

scended and maintained, then entré into one area of inquiry tends to a greater chance of further entré.[4]

The Systematic Collection of Data

For the apprentice who emerges from the phase of open, unstructured observation into a new phase where he formulates ideas about how groups tend to operate, and seeks evidence against which to check these ideas, the second procedure is to devise methods for taking disciplined readings on what occurs.[5] Methods of measurement and techniques for collecting data—if they are to be of more than transitory interest—derive from a conception of which facets of group phenomena are relevant and important both to the immediate group and to the general universe of groups. Few methods exemplify the connection between a conception of groups and a method for gathering empirical readings better than Bales' Interaction Process Analysis, one of the more cleanly devised, and certainly one of the most widely used, techniques for categorizing overt behavior in groups.[6]

Interaction Process Analysis

Each overt act that occurs in a group is classified in one of the 12 categories shown in Table 1. The boiling-down of all possible ways of interpreting group events into this set is a product of a highly ordered conception of group processes; some main features are paraphrased as follows:

1. The small, face-to-face group is one instance of a more general type of system (the social system) which includes organizations, communities, societies, and nations. As such, the small group possesses many features comparable to features found in social systems, such as an organization of activities, differential contact among members, division of labor, norms and means of social control, power structure, sub-groups, ideology, ceremonies, and patterned means for coping with both internal and external problems.

2. The origin of these features and their dynamic relation may be studied relatively simply in the small group, not only because groups are relatively easy to observe but because the structural features (such as a division of labor or a given power structure) are solutions to issues arising out of a specific context of interaction. Through detailed study of the interaction process one is able to identify such issues, to specify the group's response to them, and consequently to account for the structural features of the system. The more detailed the anal-

[4] The issues in becoming an observer of small groups are paralleled in the general sociologist's relation to societies. They are discussed in the latter context by Edward Shils, in "The Calling of Sociology," in Talcott Parsons, Edward Shils, Kaspar D. Naegele, and Jesse R. Pitts (eds.), Theories of Society, Vol. II (New York: The Free Press of Glencoe, 1961), pp. 1405–1448.

[5] For an early review of observation schemes see Roger W. Heyns and Ronald Lippitt, "Systematic Observation Techniques," in Gardner Lindzey (ed.), Handbook of Social Psychology, Vol. I (Cambridge: Addison-Wesley, 1954), pp. 370–404; and for a review of more recent techniques, see Karl E. Weick, "Systematic Observation Methods," in Gardner Lindzey and Elliot Aronson (eds.), Handbook of Social Psychology, rev. ed. (forthcoming).

[6] Bales, Interaction Process Analysis. For examples of the application of Bales' method see George A. Talland, "Task and Interaction Process: Some Characteristics of Therapeutic Group Discussion," Journal of Abnormal and Social Psychology (1955), L: 105–109; George Psathas, "Phase Movement and Equilibrium Tendencies in Interaction Process Analysis in Psychotherapy Groups," Sociometry (June 1960), XXIII: 177–194; and H. Lennard and A. Bernstein, The Anatomy of Psychotherapy: Systems of Communication and Expectation (New York: Columbia University Press, 1960).

observation

Table 1

Bales' Set of Observation Categories

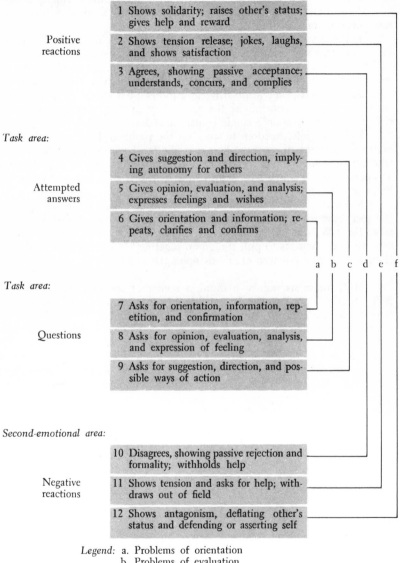

Social-emotional area:

Positive reactions

1 Shows solidarity; raises other's status; gives help and reward

2 Shows tension release; jokes, laughs, and shows satisfaction

3 Agrees, showing passive acceptance; understands, concurs, and complies

Task area:

Attempted answers

4 Gives suggestion and direction, implying autonomy for others

5 Gives opinion, evaluation, and analysis; expresses feelings and wishes

6 Gives orientation and information; repeats, clarifies and confirms

a b c d e f

Task area:

Questions

7 Asks for orientation, information, repetition, and confirmation

8 Asks for opinion, evaluation, analysis, and expression of feeling

9 Asks for suggestion, direction, and possible ways of action

Second-emotional area:

Negative reactions

10 Disagrees, showing passive rejection and formality; withholds help

11 Shows tension and asks for help; withdraws out of field

12 Shows antagonism, deflating other's status and defending or asserting self

Legend: a. Problems of orientation
b. Problems of evaluation
c. Problems of control
d. Problems of decision
e. Problems of tension-management
f. Problems of integration

Adapted with permission from Robert F. Bales, "A Set of Categories for the Analysis of Small Group Interaction," *American Sociological Review* (1950), XV: 257–263.

ysis of process, the clearer it becomes that the structural features and interaction process are simply two aspects of the same phenomenon.

3. A wide range of interpersonal encounters can usefully be conceived as problem-solving. When people meet, there are differences to be ironed out and decisions to be made—whether the occasion is an argument among roommates, a family at dinner, a community meeting, a university seminar, a board of directors' meeting, or a council of war.

4. If a group is to solve its problems and arrive at its decisions, certain basic functions must be performed at a minimum level of proficiency: (a) *communication:* through exchange of information, members must arrive at a common definition of the situation they confront; (b) *evaluation:* through exchange of ideas and opinions, they must arrive at a more-or-less shared attitude toward the situation; and (c) *control:* in the face of competing alternatives, they must choose and decide upon a single course of action.

5. Meanwhile, freedom to work on the problem depends on certain interpersonal processes: there must be a periodic feedback from members, indicating whether movement of the group in a particular direction is acceptable or unacceptable; the tension level within and between members must not get too high; and the group must be held together.

6. Finally, Bales suggests that the instrumental functions in 4 above, and the socio-emotional functions in 5 above, are dynamically related: attempts to solve the task tend to break up the group, thereby necessitating reintegrative activity; and attempts to pull the group together tend to weaken task efficiency, thereby requiring renewed emphasis upon the task.

With these six points in mind, a review of the 12 categories shows that Bales' method employs the fewest possible categories in order to collect data relevant to the concept. Acts primarily relevant to the problem of communication are classified in either category 6 or 7; those relevant to evaluation, in either category 5 or 8; those relevant to control, or decision, in either category 4 or 9. Reactions to these instrumental attempts which facilitate forward movement are classified in the "green-light" set (category 3 when an agreement to a statement, category 2 when a sign of tension-reduction, and category 1 when a manifestation of interpersonal or group solidarity). Reactions which impede forward movement or which indicate resistance to that movement are classified in the "red-light" set (category 10 if a disagreement to a statement, category 11 if a sign of increased tension, and category 12 if a manifestation of hostility toward a person or the group as a whole).

The scoring procedure is simple: the observer (1) gives each group member an arbitrary number; (2) screens each act or gesture to determine which of the functions it is most directly relevant to; (3) records the act by placing it in the appropriate category, indicating both the number of the person initiating it and the number of the person to whom it is directed; and (4) continues this procedure as acts occur, keeping scores in an order corresponding to their occurrence (and often using as an aid a machine with a moving tape).

With training and considerable practice, and after having scored process in a given set of groups, the apprentice may arrange his data in order to answer the following types of questions:

1. Does interaction follow an ordered sequence—for example, from the beginning to the end of a meeting? Bales and Strodtbeck suggest a general, and ideal, sequence wherein instrumental emphasis shifts first from problems of

32

observation

communication to problems of evaluation, and finally to problems of control.[7]

2. Is there a dynamic relation, or covariation, between task activity and socio-emotional activity? Again Bales and Strodtbeck suggest that as the group moves through problems of communication, evaluation, and control, "red-light" activity will increase, and that after the point of decision and as a manifestation of consolidation, "green-light" categories will increase.[8]

3. Is there a pattern in the distribution of interpersonal interaction? Is the communication network structured? Bales and associates have collected evidence suggesting a tendency for each actor to distribute his action among others according to their output, resulting in a network wherein the relative frequency of acts between any two parties can be estimated by their total output relative to other members.[9]

4. How do members divide among themselves the performance of the various behavioral functions represented by the categories? Slater and Bales find a tendency, under certain conditions, for one active member to push toward solving the problem while the other active member attempts to hold the group together—a division of functions corresponding to the major distinctions among the categories and, accordingly, to the basic functional problems outlined in Bales' original formulation.[10]

5. Conceiving of the interaction process as a more-or-less ordered system changing through time, what variables affect the characteristics of this system? Here the apprentice may be led in any one of a number of directions. For example, consider the effect that the following factors would have: the kind of problem the group is working on; the personalities of the members, taken individually and as a configuration; the size of the group; sex, age, and social class of members; age of the group; relation of the group to other groups, and its relation to the observer. One could extend the list, but the question remains essentially the same—namely: If we view the overt interpersonal behavioral process as the result of the convergence of a number of forces at a particular time and place, what factors affect those forces which, in turn, alter in a determinate way the interaction process?

Other Dimensions of Group Process

The value of Bales' method to the apprentice goes beyond the data produced. First, it sharpens his eye and disciplines him to attend to each event that occurs. Though he may score only one aspect of each act, he leaves out no acts. Second, the method introduces a conception of the ongoing interaction system, the problem-solving aspect of which is clearly formulated and rationally connected to the scoring operation. The good scorer employs this conception and, as he improves his scoring, tends to refine his own conception of the system. With the conception of the system on one hand and the appearance of an event on the other, the scoring operation is, in the end, a judgment about what each event does to the system. In making such judgments the apprentice

[7] Robert F. Bales and Fred L. Strodtbeck, "Phases in Group Problem Solving," *Journal of Abnormal and Social Psychology* (1951), XLVI: 485–495.

[8] *Ibid.*

[9] Robert F. Bales, Fred L. Strodtbeck, Theodore M. Mills, and Mary E. Roseborough, "Channels of Communication in Small Groups," *American Sociological Review* (1951), XVI: 461–468.

[10] Robert F. Bales and Philip E. Slater, "Role Differentiation in Small Decision-Making Groups," in Talcott Parsons, Robert F. Bales, *et al.*, *The Family, Socialization and Interaction Process* (New York: The Free Press of Glencoe, 1955), pp. 259–306.

tends to become more keenly aware of the intricate patterns and ordered sequences that characterize interaction. Like the student of music who learns an orchestral score, he begins to comprehend the design underlying its interaction; the sensing of a "score" by the apprentice tends to open to him a new world of interpersonal process. Third, Bales' method does not try to capture the richness of all these processes. From the full score, as it were, it abstracts one line: it selects the problem-solving relevance of activity, leaving other dimensions, or other lines in the score, to other methods. The value to the apprentice is that what is picked up and what is not picked up is clearly and unambiguously formulated. Consequently, Bales' method throws into sharp relief the untouched dimensions which require special methods of their own. Some of these follow.

1. The substantive *content* of statements: the ideas that are conveyed
2. The intent of the actor: the aim, purpose, or motivation behind actions
3. Feelings experienced by others, as well as the actor, while someone is acting
4. Thoughts in the minds of members stimulated or evoked by the action, such as: Is what is going on good or bad, appropriate or inappropriate, effective or ineffective, desirable or undesirable?

Sociologists interested in "what is said"—interested in classifying the types of ideas, in tracing their order of appearance, in registering their acceptance, rejection, or modification, and in following their accumulation as part of group culture—such sociologists require a separate scheme especially designed to abstract the *content* line of the "score." One example of such a method is Mills' Sign Process Analysis; [11] another is *The General Inquirer*, which uses uses language translation techniques to select and to simplify the content, and the modern computer to speed up categorization, storing, ordering, and retrieval.[12] When an investigator combines data from one of these methods with data from Interaction Process Analysis, he has information on both "what is said" (inputs to group culture) and on the action's effect upon the problem-solving system. Therefore, he may explore in the small group an aspect of one of the classical issues of sociology; namely, the dynamic relation between culture and social structure. For example, does change in a person's expressed ideas affect his position in the group? Does a shift on the part of the group as a whole from one type of thought to another affect the distribution of interaction? Are there structures of interaction that restrict the realm of expressible thought? Are there others that expand the realm? Investigation of this type of issue is a second step in the dynamic analysis of group process. There are additional ones.

Beneath the overt act lie covert feelings, and behind the explicit statement are unexpressed thoughts. Beyond this, the overt act and the explicit statement. evoke in other members feelings and thoughts, a large proportion of which are not clearly manifest—at least not to the ear and to the eye we are accustomed to use in observing groups. This means that much of the iceberg of group process is below the surface: feelings of pleasure or displeasure; wishes to affirm or to disaffirm; evaluations of others as good or bad, and of their actions as appropriate or inappropriate; and so on. These processes, howsoever covert, are potentially important. Assuming that they are possible causal factors and that they can become known through reliable empirical indicators, the sociologist

[11] Theodore M. Mills, *Group Transformation* (Englewood Cliffs, N. J.: Prentice-Hall, 1964), pp. 19–41.
[12] Philip J. Stone, Dexter C. Dunphy, Marshall S. Smith, and Daniel M. Ogilvie, *The General Inquirer: A Computer Approach to Content Analysis* (Cambridge: M.I.T. Press, 1966).

observation

needs a new type of method. He needs techniques which help him become aware of the existence of these processes and which assist him in deciphering what we must assume to be the subtle signals through which they are manifest, whether those signals turn out to be linguistic, kinesic, physiological, or otherwise. At present, such techniques are in their infancy. In fact, their development is one of the frontiers of small-groups research.[13]

Anticipating the time when such methods are available, we can appreciate not only the value of the clear distinction made by Bales, but the advantage of applying a number of observational methods simultaneously. This advantage accrues because the investigator may use a bank of observers, each employing a method that taps a separate dimension: one may classify content; another, problem-solving relevance; another, feelings; another, the relationship between activity and the rules; yet another, the relation between activity and group values. With independent but simultaneous readings on these analytically distinct dimensions, the investigator will be able to extend his study to an even more general sociological issue—namely, the dynamic principles that relate (1) interaction, (2) cultural content, (3) emotional processes, (4) rules and norms, and (5) beliefs and values. First, are there such principles? If so, are they uniform from one group to another, or are there different sets of principles for different types of groups? Are such principles constant throughout the life of a group, or do they alter as the group forms, develops, performs its purpose, and then disbands? This issue parallels major theoretical and empirical concerns of historians, sociologists, and anthropologists who study the dynamics of larger organizations, societies, and nations. Progress on the issue in the small-group setting depends heavily upon the development of systematic techniques for collecting empirical readings on the configurations of covert thoughts and feelings associated with overt action.

Interim Measures

In the absence of a full repertoire of techniques, the small-group researcher resorts to cross-sectional estimates—to readings taken at the end of a session or between meetings. By means of questionnaires, tests, interviews, and similar devices, he elicits *ex post facto* responses from members about their thoughts and feelings, and attempts to piece together a picture of the submerged part of the aforementioned "iceberg." Some examples of such post-session data-collecting techniques follow.

1. *Sociometric Questions.* The investigator asks members such questions (and gives such instructions) as: "Of the persons here today, whom do you like most? Rank-order all members according to your liking for them"; or, "With whom would you most like to spend a sociable evening? Rank all members according to your preference"; or, "The group will face a very difficult and frustrating task which must be performed by pairs. Whom would you prefer to have work with you? Rank all persons according to your preference." Examination of such

---

[13] See R. L. Birdwhistell, *Introduction to Kinesics* (Louisville: University of Louisville Press, 1952); George F. Mahl, "Exploring Emotional States by Content Analysis," in Ithiel De Sola Pool (ed.), *Trends in Content Analysis* (Urbana: University of Illinois Press, 1959), pp. 89–130; A. T. Ditman and Lyman C. Wynne, "Linguistic Techniques and the Analysis of Emotionality in Interviews," *Journal of Abnormal and Social Psychology* (1961), LXIII: 201–204; Robert E. Pettinger, Charles F. Hockett, and John J. Danely, *The First Five Minutes* (Ithaca, N. Y.: Paul Martineau, 1960); and R. G. Barker, *The Stream of Behavior* (New York: Appleton-Century, 1963).

preferences provides first approximations to configurations of interpersonal feelings and evaluations.[14]

2. *Projective Pictures.* The investigator asks the group to perform a special task for him, which is to work together in creating dramatic stories about pictures of groups which he presents to them one at a time. The group is free to develop any story it chooses; the theme, the main characters, the outcome, and so on are left up to them. Assuming that groups, like persons responding to ink blots, project into the story latent processes which they are not otherwise free to convey, the investigator infers certain group characteristics from the ideas presented, from the nature of the main characters, and from the story's theme and outcome. He may infer, for example, the underlying emotional state of the group, its latent conflicts, its degree of disorganization, and its sense of solidarity. Since the precise connections between latent processes and collectively produced themes are still in question, this device is at present more exploratory and suggestive than definitive.[15]

3. *Member Ratings.* The investigator asks members to rate one another using various criteria, exemplified in such questions (and instructions) as: "Who was most helpful in getting the problem solved? Rank all members including yourself"; or, "Who was most helpful in holding the group together and in resolving the interpersonal problems that arose? Rank all members, including yourself"; or, "Who seemed most aware of what was going on during the session?"—and so on, through a list of assessments. From such responses the investigator forms a first approximation to the configuration of definitions members have of one another, and to the values they place upon what they do.[16]

4. *Individual Interviews.* In order to understand the meaning of the group experience to members, the investigator meets with each one privately, asking him a variety of questions ranging from the quite open-ended ones such as "How would you describe what happened today?" or "What impressed you most in the session?" to more specific ones, such as: "When John left the room and Henry heaved his great sigh, what were your feelings? Why did you think John left? How did you think Henry felt? What effect did John's leaving have upon the group?"—and so on. From such open-ended questions the investigator attempts to learn where in the person's life-space the group experience is located (*i.e.*, its importance to him, his involvement in it, and so on), and from answers of members to specific questions, the investigator gauges the similarities and differences in their feelings about and attitudes toward selected events.[17]

---

[14] For a discussion of the various types of sociometric questions, their application, and ways of analyzing the data they provide, see Gardner Lindzey and Edgar F. Borgatta, "Sociometric Measurement," in Lindzey (ed.), *Handbook of Social Psychology*, pp. 405–448; also see A. Paul Hare, *Handbook of Small Group Research* (New York: The Free Press of Glencoe, 1962), pp. 407–411.

[15] William E. Henry and Harold Guetzkow, "Group Projective Sketches for the Study of Small Groups," *Journal of Social Psychology* (1951), XXXIII: 77–102; M. Horwitz and Dorwin Cartwright, "A Projective Method for the Diagnosis of Group Properties," *Human Relations* (1953), VI: 397–410; and Theodore M. Mills, "Developmental Processes in Three Person Groups," *Human Relations* (1956), IX: 343–354.

[16] For an illustrative example, see Philip E. Slater, "Role Differentiation in Small Groups," in Hare, Borgatta, and Bales (eds.), *Small Groups*, pp. 498–515.

[17] Eleanor E. Maccoby and Nathan Maccoby, "The Interview: A Tool of Social Science," in Lindzey (ed.), *Handbook of Social Psychology*, pp. 449–487; for a comparison of the use of the interview and questionnaires see Claire Sellitz, Marie Jahoda, Morton Deutsch, and Stuart W. Cook. (eds.), *Research Methods in Social Relations*, rev. ed. (New York: Dryden, 1959), pp. 236–268.

36

5. *Group Interviews.* In order to understand the group's collective reaction to what it has collectively done, to assess the group's capacity for reviewing and evaluating its own process, to see how it presents itself to an outside investigator, and to compare its operation when evaluating itself with its operation when working on other types of tasks, the investigator asks the group to meet in special session with him, wherein he raises for general discussion questions similar to those in the individual interview.

Although these five types of post-session devices provide a first approximation to the subjective experience of group members, they are inadequate for the full dynamic analysis ˦ entioned above because the responses they evoke are restrospective, compressed, and directly influenced by the outside investigator. Being given after the discussions they are, of course, affected by the total experience and by its outcome. Beyond this, they usually compress, into a single answer, a variety of experiences. For example, when in the course of a meeting one member's attitude toward another member changes from approval to disapproval, and then to indifference, and when after the meeting he reports that he is indifferent to him, that report leads the investigator to a simplified and erroneous conclusion about the relation between these two persons. The conclusion can not explain how change in behavior is related to change in evaluations. Furthermore, since all reports of fellow members are compressed in this manner, and since there is no way of knowing precisely what stimulated the reports, what appears as similarity in response, or consensus, may be no more than a set of responses about different stimuli. And, of course, existing consensus may not appear at all because, again, members refer to different events when they give their reports. The difficulty arises because the events which stimulate the subjective responses are unknown.

Selected replay is a technique designed to reduce the compression of post-session responses: by means of a sound or video tape-recording, the investigator replays a series of episodes selected from the previous interaction. He asks members at the end of each episode to report as nearly as possible the feelings, ideas, and other reactions they experienced when the episode occurred. This method enables the investigator to determine the cross-sectional configuration of subjective responses throughout the group for each discrete episode, and consequently to trace the changes in configuration through time, whether the change be toward or away from consensus, toward the isolation of a single member, toward a schism, or toward some other formation of interest to him. Though the method reduces the ambiguity of post-session responses by tying responses to specific events, those responses, of course, remain retroactive.[18]

All post-session responses are influenced by the fact that they are given to an outsider. Although not enough is known about this influence, from the viewpoint of an analysis of what happens *in* the group, it must be assumed to be an error factor until demonstrated otherwise.

In summary, there are practical methods for collecting systematic data on the more overt dimensions of group process, such as interaction and content; and there are techniques for eliciting members' post-session responses. If the sociology of groups is to achieve a more comprehensive dynamic analysis, these methods need to be supplemented with workable techniques for detecting and assessing the continuous but largely covert emotional, evaluative, and ideational processes.

[18] Theodore M. Mills, Hope Leichter, and Gene C. Kassabaum, "Frankness and Consensus: An Approach to Covert Group Processes," Interaction Laboratory, Yale University, mimeographed.

Collaboration between Observer and Group

If the first procedure of the sociologist is to gain access to the group without undermining it, and if the second is to devise a set of methods for assessing the various dimensions of group process, then a third procedure, which contributes to both of these, is for the investigator and the group to come together again. This reconvening is done in order both that the group may learn about itself from the investigator, and that he may reassess the meaning, relevance, and importance of his data to groups. We conclude this chapter with an outline of the development of a social relation between investigator and group which permits the optimal use of information in the setting for the benefit of the group, the investigator, and the advancement of the sociology of groups. Toward this ideal there are six steps, represented by six questions to which either a "no" or a "yes" answer can be given for any given study. When a "no" answer is appropriate, then the social relation in that particular study has been blocked or deflected from a more productive course, while when a "yes" answer for all questions is appropriate, then the relation approaches the ideal.

1. Does the sociologist contact existing groups, asking their consent to be observed?

No: for example, either because
   a. He chooses to use secondary sources in studying groups; or because
   b. He doubts the legitimacy of his right to ask for access or to interfere with their procedures; or because
   c. Even though he feels his cause is legitimate, he anticipates refusal and wants to avoid being rejected; or because of related reasons— *but, in any case,* groups are not asked to be observed. (In this connection an interesting comparison would be between the types of groups that are most apt to be contacted and those that are least apt to be contacted.)

Yes: He makes contact and seeks access.

2. If contact is made, then does the group grant access to its processes with a sufficient sense of confidence and trust?

No: for example, either because
   a. It fears that the presence of an outsider will raise problems it is unable to cope with; or because
   b. It believes that granting access would endanger its relationships to other persons or groups to which it is responsible, or because
   c. Even though it grants access, perhaps through the orders of superiors or in response to other external pressures, it represses, suppresses, and otherwise censors information conveyed to the observes; or because of related reasons— *but, in any case,* the accessibility of the investigator is partial and limited.

Yes: The group grants the observer the privilege of observing it.

3. If accessibility is granted, then do the two parties, group and observer, respond to one another so that their separate goals and their integrity in pursuing those goals are respected?

38

observation

No: for example, either because
  a. The observer feels discomfort in observing and leaves the situation; or because
  b. He, being drawn into the group, departs' from the role of scientist (as for example the observer of the industrial firm becomes an organizational executive, or the observer of therapy groups decides to become either a therapist or a patient); or because
  c. The group, feeling more vulnerable than it anticipated, extends its jurisdiction over the observer, demanding the right to know all that he is doing, thinking, and learning, and to censor what he reports to others; or because of related reasons—
     but, in any case, the two parties are unable to be both together and independent.
Yes: The observer and the group coexist, each pursuing its separate task while being in contact with the other.

4. If observer and group coexist, do they exchange observations, interpretations, and feelings about what is happening? In other words, do they provide one another with feedback?

No: for example, because
  a. The observer, being uncertain of the relevance and value of his readings to the group, keeps them to himself; or because
  b. Though he feels obligated to report data to scientific colleagues, he feels no obligation toward the layman or toward the groups he observes; or because
  c. He believes the persons observed have nothing of value to add to his own observations and interpretations; or because
  d. The group is not interested in what the observer learns or, if it is, it is reluctant to initiate an exchange, or for other reasons—
     but, in any case, persons (members and observer) who have been exposed to the same events, though from different viewpoints, do not take the opportunity to learn from each other.
Yes: for example,
  a. The observer reports his observations to the group and re-interprets their meaning by judging its reaction to them. What is accepted, what is denied, what seems strange, what seems clear—all these are taken as new readings about the nature of the group and, of course, may be fed back immediately for another round of reactions;
  b. Meanwhile, the group judges the viewpoint and the perceptivity of the observer through what he selects, misses, emphasizes and minimizes and, in view of their assessment, instructs him further on their experience as they see it.
  c. Through such an exchange the different viewpoints are brought to light, the relation between group and observer is clarified and an additional framework for interpreting the original observations appears.

5. If there is reciprocal feedback, then does each party "take the role of the other," in the sense that each incorporates some of the functions of the other?

No:

    a. The functions of *participating* and of *observing participation* remain divided between insiders and outsiders: members leave objective observation and serious interpretation to outsiders, while the observer remains intellectually detached from the groups he observes;

    b. The group becomes a "client" of technical, expert observers possibly going from one expert to another, while the observer becomes a consultant, in his case, going from client to client.

In passing and as an example of a "yes" answer to the question, we may note that self-analytic groups, referred to in the introduction, are a modern sociological invention in which traditional conceptions of group boundaries are altered and consciously redrawn. The outside observer's function is incorporated by the group. In addition to participating, members observe their own actions. Consequently, "detached" observation becomes part of the immediate feedback process. At the same time "the observer," being a member, can act immediately on his observations. Therefore, he can make direct empirical tests of the accuracy, relevance, and importance of his observations. As a result, responses to his observations become part of the feedback process. By integrating observation and participation within the purpose of the single group, the self-analytic group is, in this sense, a significant forward step in transcending the boundary between observer and group.

6. If the parties acquire functions from one another, do they convey what they have learned, and export their new capabilities to persons and groups beyond the immediate context?

No: for example, because

    a. The observer, believing the case to be unique, does not compare this group with others, or test his ideas on other groups; or because

    b. The observer, believing the findings to be of limited relevance to other groups and observers, does not publish his experience or, if he does, restricts his report to his original observations, unmodified by the group's response to them or by his revised frame of reference; or because

    c. The group keeps the lessons of its experience within its own circle, perhaps as a new mark of distinction, a new sign of the difference between the in-group and outsiders; or because of related reasons.

Yes:

    a. The observer formulates what he learns and how he learned it and, through publication, conference, or teaching, transmits it to others; [19] and

    b. The group, having increased its own range of observation and its skill in comprehending itself, conveys these new capabilities to others who may, as a result, become more open to observation.

       If such is the case, then we have an instance of a relation between observer and group, and an order of exchange between them which utilizes to an optimal degree the potential resources in the normal situation of group observation for advancing the scientific study of groups.

---

[19] William F. Whyte, *Street Corner Society: The Social Structure of an Italian Slum* (Chicago: University of Chicago Press, 1943).

observation

The fundamental procedural problem for the sociologist is to avoid the dead ends represented under the *No* headings above and, in the long run, to devise those features suggested by items under the *Yes* headings. The course represented by *Yes* answers promises to extend both the degree of intimate contact with group phenomena, and the range of phenomena about which systematic data may be collected.

experimentation

three

The experimental method enjoys a definite advantage over observation and description. Through an example, this chapter notes this advantage, points to certain dynamic effects of manipulating group variables, and, following the lead of the previous chapter, outlines an optimal working relation between experimenter and groups. But before we get deeply into our discussion, let us consider a few simple facts basic to it.

Obviously, the discovery through observation (in any discipline you might care to mention) that one variable is associated with another may be considered a gainful advance in that field of knowledge. However, the question remains as to whether change in one of the variables is both a necessary and a sufficient condition for change in the second. For example, suggesting associations between such things as altitude and barometer readings, climate and malaria, business activity and suicide, frustration and aggression, and democratic leadership and satisfaction is no proof of what causes the barometer's change, malaria, suicide, aggression, and group satisfaction. If, while holding other things constant, one were able to alter one variable and observe change or lack of change in the other, then one could begin to determine "causes." And if, through a series of tests, one were able to alter one variable after the other, one might eventually discover variables or sets of variables to which change in the second one is most sensitive—the study of malaria being a case in point.

We begin to see, then, that, compared to observation and description, the experimental method is highly efficient both in eliminating apparently reasonable but inadequate hypotheses, and in indicating those hypotheses that cannot easily be rejected. And experimentation proves itself of particular value in such special circumstances as dealing with two theories, one predicting an opposite outcome from the other, for then the experiment tests an entire body of thought.[1] Though attractive because of its efficiency and potential power for resolving theoretical issues, the experimental method is not practical or even possible for many investigators. For example, the modern astronomer still cannot shift heavenly bodies at will in order to observe the effects of such shifts. Instead, he must wait for an eclipse, or for the visit of a comet, to conduct his experiments. Only recently has he been able to take readings from beyond the earth's atmosphere and to plan experiments within the solar system. The struggle to obtain more accurate readings of the heavens and to be able to introduce known variations in space has been going on since ancient times. So we see that physical realities continue to limit the use of the experimental method in this particular science, and much the same applies to other fields. The astronomer's counterpart in social science is, as we shall see, limited more frequently by the realities of moral restraints and of human sensitivities.

To experiment on communities or nations—for example, to test the effects of a change in technology, or a change in the legal structure, or a change in the form of government—requires the very special freedom of "playing with" individual and collective life. Traditionally, that freedom is granted only to those who assume political responsibility both for their own acts and for the society on which they act. The implicit rule is: "Whosoever exercises power over us must do so—or we must have reason to believe is doing so—primarily for *our* sake. Life and society are too precious to be risked simply for the sake of a scientist's abstract ideas." Perhaps the rule was felt stronger in those societies where the traditions were not threatened by rapid changes of circumstances. In many societies during the last century in particular it has become increasingly clear that the traditional ways, including ways of learning about the self and society, are inadequate and that leaders, whether of nations or of very small groups, need better information on and a clearer grasp of social processes. Partly because of the possibility that social science can evaluate our folk-beliefs about how groups *should* operate by examining and testing how they *do* operate, the moral restraint on experimentation is gradually lessening. Then, too, the restraint is undoubtedly less for small groups than for societies, and probably even less for individuals than for groups. In any case, the twentieth century in social science is marked by a rapid increase in experimentation. Not the least important was the hope on the part of such men as Kurt Lewin that we might be able both to locate specific causes of group phenomena and to test beyond reasonable doubt some of our basic ideas about groups.

Through Lewin's influence, Lippitt and White were aware of the possibilities of experimentation when they tested the effects of leadership styles upon

[1] On the logic of experimentation see Claire Sellitz, Marie Jahoda, Morton Deutsch, and Stuart W. Cook (eds.), *Research Methods in Social Relations*, rev. ed. (New York: Dryden, 1959), pp. 80–143; on the strategy of laboratory experimentation see Leon Festinger, "Laboratory Experiments," in Leon Festinger and Daniel Katz (eds.), *Research Methods in the Behavioral Sciences* (New York: Holt, Rinehart and Winston, 1953), pp. 138–172; on experiments with groups in the field, see John R. P. French, Jr., "Experiments in Field Settings," in Festinger and Katz (eds.), *Research Methods in the Behavioral Sciences*, pp. 98–135; for types of experiments, see E. Greenwood, *Experimental Sociology, a Study in Method* (New York: King's Crown, 1945); and for functions of experiments see Abraham Kaplan, *The Conduct of Inquiry, Methodology for Behavioral Science* (San Francisco: Chandler, 1964), pp. 126–170.

43

experimentation

groups of boys.[2] In one set of groups an adult took the part of an autocratic leader; in another, the part of a democratic leader; while in a third, the part of a *laissez-faire* leader. After a period in one group, leaders shifted groups, and in some cases shifted their leadership style. By comparing measures on a number of variables covering the boys' reactions when dealing with a particular leader-style, the investigators were able to examine systematically the effects of the three styles. Since these styles are related to folk-beliefs about how groups *should* be led, the experiment, of course, has implications for our ideology as well as for the researchers' hypotheses. Quite apart from the results, this experiment demonstrated the feasibility of training persons to act a certain way, of introducing them into groups, and of testing the effects of their performance upon other processes in those groups.

Another feature was controlled and varied by Bavelas and his associates.[3] It is perhaps common knowledge that not everyone in organizations has equal access to information—that information is channeled through a network, with some persons at certain intersections receiving and giving more than others. With the supposition in mind that a relationship must exist between the pattern of such networks and the capability of organizations to solve problems, Bavelas set up laboratory groups of five persons each in which he varied the configuration of communication channels (for example, from the "circle" pattern where each person can get in touch with his two neighbors but with no one else, to the pattern where four persons can communicate with a central person but not with each other), gave the groups identical problems to solve, then measured the speed and accuracy of their solutions. Later, by varying the types of problems (from those requiring an accumulation of information to those requiring insight), the investigators suggested a three-way relation between type of network, type of problem, and degree of efficiency.[4] Again, apart from the results, the experiments demonstrated that it was possible to establish in the laboratory, and to alter with relative ease, such a complex group feature as the network of interpersonal communication.

While these and other experiments of the period inspired an impressive list of laboratory tests, some social scientists doubted their value. "Yes," it was said, "experiments are *possible*, but are they relevant? To what extent can findings obtained in the artificial world of the laboratory from *ad hoc* groups that work on unrealistic problems be generalized to the real world outside?" [5] Though we cannot enter that debate in this book, it should be noted, first, that the problem common to all experimenters, regardless of their field of science, is precisely to spell out the transposition equations according to which results obtained in one context can be usefully applied in another (the readings on an ammeter and lightning in the heavens being a case in point); and, second, that a positive way to discover those equations is to conduct experiments, and in each

[2] Ronald Lippitt, "An Experimental Study of the Effect of Democratic and Authoritarian Group Atmospheres," *University of Iowa Studies in Child Welfare* (1940), XVI: 43–195, condensed version published as Ronald Lippitt and Ralph K. White, "An Experimental Study of Leadership and Group Life," in Guy E. Swanson, Theodore M. Newcomb, and Eugene L. Hartley (eds.), *Readings in Social Psychology*, rev. ed. (New York: Holt, 1952), pp. 340–355.

[3] Dorwin Cartwright and Alvin Zander (eds.), *Group Dynamics*, 2nd ed. (Evanston: Row, Peterson, 1960), pp. 669–682.

[4] Swanson, Newcomb, and Hartley (eds.), *Readings in Social Psychology*, 2nd ed., pp. 108–125.

[5] See Guy E. Swanson, "Some Problems of Laboratory Experiments with Small Populations," *American Sociological Review* (1951), XVI: 349–358; and Lewis A. Coser, "The Functions of Small Group Research," *Social Problems* (Winter 1955–1956), III: 1–6.

experimentation

case try to bridge the gap between phenomena inside the laboratory and phenomena outside.

This chapter suggests that part of the problem is due to the fact that the experimenter acts *on* the group. In moving from observation to experimentation, the investigator shifts from passive to active: from simply observing a change to inducing a change; from taking groups as they are to introducing actors into them; from observing existing groups to creating them for his own purpose. The experimenter's dilemma is that the more he does *to* the group, the less he knows what it would be, do, or become without his interference. By experimenting, not only does he perform functions which are ordinarily performed by members themselves, but the tighter his controls and the more careful his manipulation, the less the opportunity for the group to develop on its own—and consequently, the greater his difficulty in transposing findings from such groups to more autonomous groups outside.

The present chapter suggests a dual strategy: first, for the experimenter to reexamine his relation to the group, including the meaning he has to members, the functions he performs for it, and the impact of his manipulations upon it; and second, for him to devise a collaborative relation with the group. Just as in the previous chapter it is argued that greater familiarity depends upon the observer's social relation with the group, it is argued here that extending experimentation to cover more autonomous groups depends upon a relationship wherein the group voluntarily grants him the right to manipulate it while he grants it the freedom to maintain or to develop its independence. A prospectus for such a relationship is presented at the end of the chapter. Meanwhile, let us consider why and how experiments on groups are done.

The Origin of an Experiment
For illustration, let us return to the apprentice who for several months has been observing a group of 10 male students who meet for discussion two hours each week to improve their understanding of group process, particularly in their own group. Previous topics have included: "What Is the Group's Real Purpose?"; " 'Masking,' 'Passing,' and 'Authenticity' in Presenting Oneself to Others"; and "The Moral Issues in Civil Disobedience."

Thirty minutes before the end of a November session, the observer is surprised to see John, an active and articulate member, rise from his chair, say, "Well, I have to leave," and then go.

Harry: Good luck, John!
Bob: Where's he going?
Harry: Being interviewed for medical school.

The observer recalls that before the departure the group was discussing "silences," and from his notes he traces the following sequence:

Phil: There are more sudden silences here than in other groups. . . .
Harry: Here you don't feel obligated to talk. Other places you have to fill in immediately to avoid the pain.
Bob: But when heavy talkers leave off, we fill in, don't we?
Phil: Here, if you break a silence you know breaking it will be analyzed.
John: Silences are uncomfortable, like disagreements. I don't feel comfortable when there is a disagreement. I try to work them out. When there's a silence, I want to jump in to fill the gap; keep it going to make everyone feel good.

45

A short silence follows.

    Peter: Yeah!

(General laughter)

> *Allen:* You're looking for confirmation. You make a point and you want a
> response, not just a blank. It was that way with me last week. . . .
> *John:* It's like having an argument with your girl. You say something nasty, and
> you want her to say something in return. . . .
> *Phil:* To take the sting out. . . .
> *John:* To take the sting out. Instead, she'll cry or walk out of the room or
> something. In a case like that, who's manipulating whom?

It was at this point that John left.

An attempt by several to draw out a silent member is interrupted by Peter,
who asks: "Are we the same group now that he's not here—now that John's
gone?" An active response to this question includes such comments as: "Everybody has a functional role, and when someone leaves, someone else takes it
over"; "We all take part of it; we all become more dominant"; "We change
more when someone leaves than when someone is absent"; "But, there were
traces of you here last time."

In the midst of the discussion Phil turns to Peter and says: "You actually
inherited John's departure and have been talking ever since!" Laughter around
the table is spotty and restrained and Harry murmurs, "Every time someone
leaves we get on this Goddamn subject!"

> *Peter:* This time there was a special reason. I felt insecure. It reminded me of
> last time, when a lot of you weren't here. I wasn't sure we were a group.
> *Allen:* Yes. There are certain roles to be performed. It's the group's identity.
> When someone leaves, his role has to be taken over, if. . . .
> *Bob:* By whom? Now, it's Peter taking over John's?
> *Dick:* Oh, you see! We have no way of talking about this! We have ruined it
> by talking about it! If you had only waited to see what would happen . . .
> but now, after two seconds, we say "Peter has John's role."

While Dick is speaking, Peter picks up his papers and with a broad smile
moves into John's chair. Harry, next to him, jokingly suggests that he put one
foot up on the table as John often does. Others watch the moves carefully. Finally, with a flourish, Peter strikes John's pose.

> *Allen:* What's going on here?
> *Peter:* Oh, well! I can't quite fill his role.
> *Harry:* You're right! You're so right! In losing John I feel like I have lost the
> king of the mountain—being alone on this side of the table. I felt I had
> to hold up this side of the table. You get security when someone is next
> to you.

"Well," says Bob to Peter, "now say something!"

Later, the apprentice reviews the sequence: discomfort over silences; analysis of the person who breaks them; the less-active filling in when talkers are
quiet; breaking a silence is like settling a disagreement; "Is the group the same
without John?"; functional roles and group identity; Peter's bodily move in
taking John's place; and Harry's comfort in having a companion.

The observer recalls similar occasions from his experience: members daring

experimentation

someone to sit in the leader's chair when he was absent; the father's instruction to the son: "Take care of the family while I'm away"; the daughter's excitement in playing mother while the mother was away; a hockey team whose star is in the penalty box; the loss of fellow soldiers on a patrol. Clearly (he thinks), when a group member leaves, others tend to fill the gap. But how general is this gap-filling phenomenon? How can it be explained? What about groups can be learned by the way they manage departures?

The apprentice formulates his first explanation of the gap-filling phenomenon as follows: Groups are in problem-solving situations. They must perform certain functions to meet situational demands. Through trial and error, members allocate among themselves activities so as to perform these functions. A departure results in a functional void, and the void incapacitates the group. To counteract this, other members, either singly or in concert, alter their own behavior. The gap is filled and the function is performed. The use of phrase, gesture, and stance of the absent person is simply a more noticeable indication of the less obvious gap-filling.

On reflection, this hypothesis is so reasonable to the apprentice that he abandons it—that is, until he is challenged by a fellow student during a seminar report. "How," he is asked, "do you know what is cause and effect? You observe the gap-filling *after* the member departs. How do you know the member does not leave because his role is being taken over? In your illustration, John said that the girl left because he had been nasty to her; and remember: just before he left, he asked, 'Who is manipulating whom?' I could argue that members, being possessive about their own functions, feel undermined when they sense others are usurping their functions, and will, if they can, leave the group before it becomes obvious that they are being displaced. By your example you can't prove that departure precedes gap-filling. Maybe being displaced precedes departure."

"But," replies the apprentice, "this can be tested experimentally: we can set up groups and pull members out according to a pre-arranged plan unknown to group members. If gap-filling follows, then there is little question."

A second student agrees to the test but suggests another reason for the gap-filling phenomenon. "Your hypothesis," he argues, "assumes that solving a problem is the primary concern, as though the most important loss to the family when the mother is away is housekeeping. The mechanism may not be so cold, rational and goal-oriented. Group members become emotionally attached to one another. When someone departs, others naturally feel an emotional loss and try to reduce it by bringing him back, by acting as he would act and by saying what he would say. I think others will fill the gap when they are fond of the person, regardless of how effective he is. I predict gap-filling when others are fond of the person, while you predict gap-filling when he is effective."

Still another view comes from a third student: "Whether the phenomenon is rational or non-rational, instrumental or affective are secondary issues. The primary point is that groups tend to maintain a state of equilibrium. Accordingly, the disturbance of a departure should be followed by a reaction tending to return the group to the state prior to his departure. While gap-filling fits this in general, the specific reaction should be in proportion to the extent of the disturbance. This means that gap-filling is correlated with the activity rate of the person who leaves. Only if he has been active—as John was in your example—will gap-filling occur. If he had been silent or passive it would not have occurred. Suppose John had been a silent member, would you expect others to be silent as a means of filling a gap?"

To complete the circle, a fourth student contends that everyone is being

47

constrained by a single illustration. "Before you go on, consider two points. First, think of all the possible factors that might effect your dependent variable, the gap-filling phenomenon. How about group size? The smaller the group, the greater the disturbance, loss, functional void, or what-have-you. How about solidarity? The more cohesive the group, the greater the loss. Just two conditions in a long list that could include personality of members, their age, their class membership, the sex composition of the group, and so on. To what universe of groups are you trying to generalize? You must take into account the variables that differentiate groups if you are to be scientifically serious about it.

"And, second," he continues, "if you want to be genuinely theoretical, why restrict yourself to departures? The general issue is change in group boundaries. You should consider the arrival of a newcomer, or at least the re-entry of the person who leaves. What mechanism operates then, and why? The newcomer, as we know, must undergo initiation in order to belong. It's just as true that the person returning must pay a readmission price, bring a gift, give a party, or present some token, even if it is no more than to tell of his travels. How do groups react to the one who returns? Do they fill him in on what has happened in his absence? Note this second type of gap and this second type of gap-filling; namely, filling each other in on all that has happened to the two parties during separation. Both gaps are associated with change in boundary. You need an hypothesis that accounts for both departure and readmission, one that specifies the necessary and sufficient conditions both for taking the absent person's place and for bringing parties up to date after separation. Unless you cover both, the more general theoretical issue of boundary change is not covered."

An Experimental Plan

Feeling that the issue is becoming too involved for open discussion, the apprentice goes to his study, works alone, and later returns with the following plan:

1. Groups with six members each meet for five two-hour sessions to work on a series of tasks including playing chess against the experimenter, debating the moral issues in civil disobedience, building a model town, interpreting a play, and inventing an automatic door-latch and release.

2. All comments are tape-recorded. At the end of each session, members rate each other on usefulness in solving the problems, and indicate whom they like and dislike.

3. Early in the fourth session the experimenter pulls one member out on a pretext, and asks the group to continue on their tasks.

4. During an intermission in the fifth session, the experimenter asks the member he pulled out to return.

The apprentice explains that the purpose of the experiment is to test the relative effects of two factors—*instrumental usefulness* and *libidinal attachment* —upon the gap-filling phenomenon.

5. There are four types of experimental groups, and a set of control groups. In control groups the experimenter pulls out no one. In experimental groups he pulls out persons according to other members' ratings of them, and their classification into four types: (1) useful and liked; (2) useful but disliked; (3) not useful but liked; and (4) not useful and disliked.

6. Each member's activity during the entire series is categorized by both Bales' *Interaction Process Analysis* and a content analysis scheme, such as The

experimentation

General Inquirer.[6] Activity before the departure is compared with activity after the departure. Changes in members' activity toward the departed person's type of activity is designated as *gap-filling activity*. In control groups, comparisons are made with persons randomly selected, since, of course, no one is pulled out.

The apprentice argues that if gap-filling activity is more frequent in experimental than in control groups, then at least departure can "cause" *gap-filling*, though of course it is still possible that displacement could cause departures. Further, he argues that if *usefulness* makes a significant difference, but libidinal attachment does not, then gap-filling is primarily an adaptive mechanism—a means of coping with the external demands; whereas, if *attachment* makes a significant difference, but not usefulness, then gap-filling is primarily an integrative mechanism—a means of reducing the group's emotional loss. If both *usefulness* and *attachment* make a difference, then gap-filling is a compound mechanism.

The equilibrium hypothesis, he continues, can be examined after the experiment, simply by testing the correlation between rate of activity of the person who is pulled out, and the volume of gap-filling activity. Finally, by asking the person to return to the group, he can compare management of re-admission with response to departures, and further explore the general issue of boundary changes.

If, when pre-tested, members do not naturally fall into the four desired categories, then the apprentice will train role-players to act out the four parts, then pull them out. If that works, then he will eventually extend his experimental program to test the effect of other factors mentioned above.

Before describing the apprentice's experience in conducting the experiment, let us review the steps in his procedures so far.

1. During unstructured observation, and quite by accident, he saw one member move into the chair of another who had departed.
2. The act brought together previous observations. Could it, he asked, be part of a more-or-less universal mechanism? He called it "the gap-filling phenomenon."
3. He formulated a tentative explanation for it.
4. Following discussions with fellow students who presented alternative hypotheses and certain methodological and theoretical problems, he reexamined his formulation.
5. Two of the hypotheses mentioned interested him. Since the choice between them could not easily be made through uncontrolled observation, he decided to test them by an experiment.
6. He designed one that would not only test these ideas but would allow him to explore the related question of readmission.
7. In short, from a chance observation he planned a major experimental program on a simple but interesting theoretical issue.

The Dynamics of Manipulation
The time is some months later and the scene is the university laboratory. The occasion is the first run of the apprentice's experiment. Since drawing up his plan, he has reviewed the relevant literature, established more precise measures of the gap-filling phenomenon, selected statistical tests to evaluate his results, and circulated questionnaires throughout the university, seeking volunteers and information on their social class, family background,

[6] Philip E. Stone, *et al., The General Inquirer* (Cambridge, Mass.: M.I.T. Press, 1966).

personality trends, attitudes, values, intelligence, peer-group associations, and so on. He has already pre-tested his experimental plan and, as he had feared, has had to change it. Since few persons in the pre-test were both effective and clearly disliked, and few were both clearly ineffective and liked, he has decided to use role-players. He has trained four associates to perform roles in groups so that they will be rated by others in one of the four classifications. His second change has arisen because not enough students have volunteered. As a result, he is obtaining his subjects through large introductory courses which require a minimum number of hours' service as an experimental subject.

As he gets the first group underway, the apprentice senses the dramatic nature of experimentation.[7] The laboratory seems a separate theatre world; the first run like opening night. The subjects under bright lights are the actors, and the observers in the dark behind the one-way mirror are the audience. The apprentice knows what it is to be producer, playwright, and director, for this is his show: he has screened and selected the actors, composed the groups, constructed the tasks, designed the questionnaires, prescribed the observations to be made and the measures to be taken. He has brought people together and will send them away. From beginning to end he has written the script—except for those few vacancies to be filled in by indicators of the dependent variable. How subjects will respond is part of the drama; a larger part is whether the experiment will work, for now it is the experimenter who is being judged. It is *he* who is now watchful, careful, and anxious.

If the session goes poorly, he is likely to discard the run, tighten up controls, and start over again. If, on the other hand, the results are clear and positive, and other groups follow suit, then he is likely to discover the strangest fact of all. On the intellectual level he will want, naturally, to check against artifacts, sleeper variables, alternative interpretations, and so on. But beyond and beneath that he discovers that *success creates a growing doubt about the reality of what has happened.* Is it, he wonders, too good to be true? Are the findings authentic? Or, with the doubt put in a more familiar way: How do the results apply to real groups in the real world outside? Might the whole production be just a play? Are the groups real or artificial; am I a scientist or a magician or am I still something else?[8]

The source of his disorientation lies not so much in the laboratory's relation to the outer world as in the experimenter's relation to the group before him. Contrast, if you will, this relation with the earlier one when he observed established groups. Earlier he was guest; now he is host. Earlier he went to the hospital or the school; now he brings subjects into his own laboratory—at best, a strange and mysterious place. Earlier he observed a persistent group; now he deals with one group after the other as they are ushered in and out. Earlier, he observed a group with internal ties of affection and currents of hostility, one with both a tradition and the power to set its own rules, one with both a purpose and the power to establish its own agenda, one with both boundaries and the power to admit and to exclude on its own; in short, an autonomous group— or at any rate autonomous enough to get along without him.

[7] On the interpersonal dynamics in experimentation see Martin T. Orne, "On the Social Psychology of the Psychological Experiment: With Particular Reference to Demand Characteristics and Their Implications," *American Psychologist* (1962), XVII: 776–783.

[8] On the consequences of the experimenter's orientation to subjects and to findings see Robert Rosenthal, "The Effect of the Experimenter on the Results of Psychological Research," in B. A. Mahr (ed.), *Progress in Experimental Personality Research*, Vol. I (New York: Academic Press, 1964), pp. 79–114.

experimentation

In contrast, the experimental group is almost wholly dependent upon him for its substance, form, and direction. Now, it is *he* who admits and excludes, *he* who assembles and dismisses, *he* who announces the purpose, sets the agenda, prescribes the rules, shifts direction, shields against outside influence, and so on—all in order properly to achieve comparable groups, standard procedures, and a reduction in experimental error. The point of the comparison is that while earlier he encountered a group that performed its own executive functions, now it is *he* who performs those functions for the group. The group literally does not know what it is until he assembles it, nor does it know what to do until he tells it.

In these circumstances the experimenter's feeling of unreality is a real response to a real contradiction—namely, that while in actuality he performs executive functions *for* the group and is, therefore, sociologically inside the group, according to scientific tradition he conceives of himself as *outside*, detached, and disinterested. While in actuality he is the group's creator, goal-setter, programmer, lawmaker, paymaster, and judge, he thinks of himself as having *no* role at all within it. More than this, he believes he *should not* have a role in it. Consequently, although an insider, he must pose as an outsider. He impersonates an outsider; he is in masquerade. As a result, he is not sure *where* he is, nor *who* he is, and things around him begin to appear unreal and artificial.

The use of deception ("Would you come with me, Mr. Brown—someone wants you on the phone.") is another part of the same theme. In proclaiming that something *is* A when it is *not* A (and in having this believed), the experimenter injects an existential proposition into the group's culture. His word *sets* the group's definition of that part of reality, much as in giving task instructions he *sets* goals and procedures. Another elaboration on the theme is the use of role-players, for to proclaim, or to imply, that these persons are *in* the group when they actually *are not* is to *set* a definition of group membership.[9]

In the meantime, what has happened to the group? As already implied, it has become a phantom, compared to what it might have become under more favorable conditions. One could present new tasks, change the rules, proclaim a new purpose—and again it would not matter, for it has become infinitely responsive, pliable, and obedient. It has become this way because when it was formed each person committed himself to the experimenter rather than to his fellow members and, basically, because the experimenter needs subjects who are willing to commit themselves primarily to him.

This phantom group is in fact the experimenter's own creation. By being playwright, producer, and director (and, we might add, by conforming closely to the prevailing practices of journeyman experimental scientists), the apprentice usurps for himself just those functions and prerogatives that the subjects themselves need if they are to develop into a genuine group. Oddly, with one hand the experimenter creates the potential for a group, but with the other takes away its means for becoming one. Quite precisely, in forming the group he gives it a form; he creates the character of his experimental subject.

This act of creating one's own subject may be peculiar to the group situation. To be sure, in recruiting a single person for an experiment, a new social *relation* between him and the experimenter is created, but we would not say a new *person* is created. However, for groups we can say just that. By bringing people together, the experimenter *creates* a group. Although it is young, indis-

9 Herbert C. Kelman, "Deception in Social Research," *Trans-action* (July/August 1966), III: 20–24.

51

tinct, and illusive, it is nonetheless a new unit with a potential for development. If this point be granted, then we may suggest that the *manner* in which persons are brought together—the way the group is conceived, if you will—makes a difference in what it can and cannot become.

Let us clarify the point by reference to the practice of recruiting subjects from courses which require participation in experiments. In such cases, the ultimate decision to enter the labroatory is not the subject's but the professor's. This fact is known to all. Those who assemble know that they are present through conscription rather than by free choice, and that therefore the act of attending is an act of compliance. Since all subjects have acted in the same way, and all subjects know each has acted in this way, their common base for group formation is compliance. This being the group's original character, only through some basic reformation could it become some other kind of group, such as an independent one. We are suggesting that investigators, in following usual procedures in setting up laboratory experiments, tend, without wishing to do so, to create partial, or phantom groups, in the sense that the groups are devoid of means for becoming independent and self-determining. The investigator is usually unaware of the degree to which he himself assumes control over the group and the extent to which he usurps just the means the group would need to become autonomous and self-determining. All this creates additional confusion in the mind of the investigator, for while under the impression that he is dealing with a group corresponding in large measure to autonomous groups outside the laboratory, he is by his own methods seriously restricting what the group might become.

To summarize: the first illusion is that the experimenter is outside the group, whereas sociologically he functions within it; the second is that the assembled aggregate is a group, whereas it is closer to a phantom, its governmental and executive powers having been taken over by the experimenter. In short, the grand illusion is that experimenter and group are *separate* systems, whereas in actuality they are *one*. They are a *single* system in which functions are divided: controlling and being controlled, setting rules and conforming to them, giving directions and obediently following them, being in charge and complying with the one in charge, being the authority and being the subordinate. Though their functions differ, the two parties constitute a single unit, a single system masquerading as two. Neither one, let us recognize, can get along without the other.

The methodological and technical problem is to conceive and to arrange, or shall we say invent, a working relationship between experimenter and group so that they may be both autonomous and interdependent. They should be *autonomous* so that the investigator, for his part, can experiment for the sake of a science, transcending both himself and the immediate group; and so that groups, for their part, have the opportunity to develop their capabilities. They should be *interdependent* in the sense that groups become prepared to give up voluntarily part of their autonomy for the sake of experimental knowledge about themselves (as well as about themselves for others); and in the sense that the experimenter becomes prepared to give up some of his controls for the sake of learning about groups with more substance. The development of such a relationship is not only desirable for the advancement of experimental sociology, it is *critical* to that advance. Without it, the investigator is reduced to testing ideas within phantom contexts. With it, there is promise not only of a wider range of groups open to experimentation but, as we shall see, of the infusion of the experimental notion into groups so that they are simply more willing to experiment on themselves.

experimentation

Collaborative Relationship
between Experimenter and Group
This chapter concludes with an outline of an optimal working relationship between experimenter and group. As with the outline in the previous chapter, there are six steps, represented by six questions to which for any given experiment either a "yes" or a "no" answer can be given. The ideal is approached when the six questions can be answered in the affirmative.

1. Does the sociologist with a testable idea and an experimental plan contact persons or groups asking them to be subjects?

No: for example, because
   a. He lacks time, space, equipment, money, and experience to carry out the project; or because
   b. He is reluctant to really test the idea empirically; or because
   c. He is uncomfortable about asking others to perform for his benefit; or because
   d. He anticipates being turned down; or for related reasons— but, *in any case*, initial contact is not made.
Yes: He makes contact and asks cooperation.

2. If contact is made, are both the groups and the experimenter willing and able to perform their parts in the experiment?

No: for example, because
   a. The subjects find the procedures too difficult, too distasteful, too boring, or morally against their scruples; or because
   b. The experimenter discovers that his plan is not feasible because there are too many loophopes, or because accurate measures cannot be made, or because the effect he wants to measure is too small; or for related reasons— but, *in any case*, the experiment aborts.
Yes: The subjects find the procedures possible, the work interesting, and the experience rewarding; the experimenter's plan is workable and he manages competently.

3. If the program is workable, then is the group's integrity as a self-governing, autonomous unit (or if it is a new group, its chances of developing into such a unit) congruent with an effective experimental test of the idea?

No: for example, because
   a. The conditions of recruitment, or the implicit contract between the parties, results in a compliant group entirely dependent upon the experimenter for guidance and direction; or because
   b. The experimenter, requiring a clear test of a single idea and comparability from group to group, takes over the group's functions of goal-setting, rule-making, and so on, rather than allowing the group to perform or to develop these functions for itself; or because
   c. The procedures demand that the group act as though it were different from what it really is—*i.e.*, that strangers be cohesive, that

students be diplomats, that a family be a committee, and so on; or for related reasons—
but, *in any case,* the group is not free to be itself and govern itself while operating in the experiment.

Yes: The self-governing group and the experimenter coexist. The group may set its own goals, make its own rules, remain or become self-governing while fulfilling the demands of the experiment, as for example when

a. The groups are newly formed and the test is upon processes of group formation; or

b. The groups are specially composed of various configurations of personalities and the test is the effect of such composition upon group formation; or

c. The groups are established (such as the family or a business firm) and the test is on how groups exercise their autonomy in the laboratory situation.

4. If self-governing (or self-developing) groups and the experimenter coexist, then do the two parties exchange information on the results and on the subjective responses to the total experimental situation? In other words, is there feedback between experimenter and group?

No: for example, because

a. The experimenter, believing members' subjective responses to be irrelevant to his purpose, does not elicit their impressions, reactions, or opinions; or because

b. During the long delay between taking the readings and interpreting their meaning, experimenter and group lose interest in, and contact with, one another; or because

c. The experimenter believes that feedback in one group would jeopardize subsequent tests in other groups; *i.e.,* the real purpose, the design, and so on, might become known prior to taking part; or because

d. The experimenter has employed deception and finds it difficult to deal openly with the group; or for other related reasons—
but *in any case,* the experimenter does not learn the group's reactions to his manipulations or its opinion about his findings, and the group does not learn about the experimenter's real purpose or about the experiment's general significance in the study of groups.

Yes: The experimenter and the group exchange reports on their experiences

a. The experimenter, for his part, elicits responses which help him gauge the importance of the total experience to the members, the revelance of the procedures to their over-all life-situation, the latent feelings they have toward him and toward one another, the implicit assumptions they have been making about the experiment's purpose, and so on—all in an attempt to assess the subjective significance of his experiment to members, and to judge its relevance to groups in general; and

b. For their part, members try to learn through the experimenter's reports more about the kind of group they are in, how it operates and how it responds to experimental treatment; and, beyond that,

experimentation

to become more fully aware of what happens in other groups they belong to.

5. If there is exchange and feedback, then do the parties "take the role of the other"? Does the group begin to experiment with itself, making changes here and there and noting their effects? Does the experimenter discover that he can work *with* groups and do something *for* them as well as do something *to* them?

No: for example,
a. The group remains dependent upon outsiders to alter its inner structure, to plan its procedures, and to set its goal; or
b. The investigator remains an experimenter-specialist (a detached laboratory-tester of hypotheses), avoiding deep involvement in any group and responsibility for applying his knowledge to existing groups.

Yes: for example,
a. The group becomes experimental; *i.e.*, it becomes better prepared to look upon its rules, goals, customs, and beliefs as tentative, and it becomes more open both to innovation and to tests of what it actually can and cannot do; and
b. The experimenter, in order to deepen his comprehension of what it means to be a person in a group, sets up and enters such groups as training or self-analytic groups (see above, p. 6 and p. 41).

6. If the parties do acquire functions modeled after one another, then do they convey to third parties—to yet others—what they have learned?

No:
a. The group becomes *avant-garde*, but ingrown. For example, with its new ideas and tricks it plays at therapy and self-analysis; and
b. The investigator becomes a private practitioner, manipulating and treating groups without publicizing his ideas, methods, or findings—
but, *in any case*, neither group nor experimenter disseminate their learning, nor train others in their capabilities.

Yes: for example,
a. The group, appreciating the value of increased self-awareness and greater flexibility in self-management, conveys these values to other persons and groups (either through informal communication or formal writings, or by being a model for them) so that they become more open to observation and experimentation; and
b. The experimenter publishes accounts of the experience, including a description of procedures (so they may be repeated), a report of results (so they may be re-tested), an interpretation of the personal and emotional significance of the experiment to subjects (so that the subjects may reconsider them), an interpretation of the theoretical significance of the findings (so it may be evaluated and criticized), and, finally, an evaluation of the strategy of the experiment.[10]

[10] For a report of an experience which approximates this sequence, yet involves only one case, see Elliott Jaques, "Social Analysis and the Glacier Project," *Human Relations* (1964), XVII: 361–375.

If those processes indicated by "yes" answers occur, then we have an instance of a social relation, and an exchange of processes between experimenter and group, which allows the optimal use of resources in the experimental situation for advancing the sociology of small groups.

Summary

An increased realization of the power of experimentation, along with an apparent relaxation of traditional restraints upon experimenting with people, have contributed to a rapid rise in the number and variety of experiments on groups. At the same time, researchers have become more acutely aware of some of the problems in such a program—in particular, the fact that the more the experimenter controls his groups, the less opportunity the group has to develop on its own and, therefore, the more difficult it is for the investigator to bridge the gap to more autonomous groups. Two courses out of this dilemma are suggested: first, a fuller understanding on the experimenter's part of what he does *to* groups when he experiments *on* them; and second, a collaborative relation between experimenter and group, wherein latitude in group development, and freedom to experiment, are questions of joint consideration.

Our review of the apprentice's experience, first as observer and then as experimenter, suggests a number of forces which tend in the first instance to press him out of the role of independent, scientific observer, and in the second to prevent the experimented-upon group from becoming self-governing. A major procedural problem in the making of a sociology of groups is to conceive of and to engineer social relations between investigator and group which reinforce their affinity and permit productive interchange.

levels
of group process:
behavior and emotion

four

This and the following three chapters present a sociological way of thinking about groups. As a first step, the present chapter divides complex interpersonal processes into five levels which have been recognized by sociologists to be different and distinct: behavior, emotions, norms, group goals, and group values.[1] It asks the reader to consider the elements on each of these levels as organized into systems, or sub-systems, each with its own features and its own principles of organization. On occasion, it also asks the reader to imagine the experience of a person who enters a group as a totally naïve newcomer but learns, through progressive stages, to operate on one level after the other until he assumes responsibility for the group as a whole and, in that capacity, operates on all five levels simultaneously. We propose that as the newcomer participates on the more advanced levels his subjective experience with the group changes, and that both the demands upon him and his potentials for contributing to the group also change. A thesis of this and the following three chapters is that as he shifts from the relatively primitive levels of behavior and emotion to the more sophisticated levels, which involve a comprehension of the group's culture and purpose, both the potential for his growth as a person and the potential for the growth of group capabilities increase.

Again, but this time more by way of definition, the five levels are as follows:

[1] Talcott Parsons and Edward A. Shils (eds.), *Toward a General Theory of Action* (Cambridge, Mass.: Harvard University Press, 1951), pp. 3–29, 53–76.

1. *Behavior:* How persons overtly act in the presence of others
2. *Emotions:* The drives persons experience, and the feelings they have toward one another and about what happens
3. *Norms:* Ideas about how persons *should* act, *should* feel, and *should* express their feelings
4. *Goals:* Ideas about what is most desirable for groups, as units, to *do*
5. *Values:* Ideas about what is most desirable for groups, as units, to *be* and to *become*

Levels one and two are discussed in this chapter; levels three and four in the next; and the fifth level is discussed in Chapter Six.

At the outset, it is important to recognize that a number of different viewpoints can be taken in interpreting group phenomena. The most common is the point of view of the single person who confronts and in some way must manage his relations with other members. We can all identify with him and not only learn from him, but in our imagination teach and coach him in the way he manages himself. Less common but nonetheless critical for the understanding of sociology is the viewpoint of one who seeks to understand what is happening to the group as a whole. What are the interpersonal dynamics? What is the course of the history of the group as a totality?

While it is true that the elements on the levels listed above are all "within the skin" of the individual or are produced by him (elements such as a drive, a feeling, an idea, or an act), it is equally true that these elements may be conceived of both as arrangements among individuals, and as constituting a social system. More specifically, one element on a given level may be considered in its relation to another element on the same level. For example, the act of one person may be considered in relation to acts of other persons, hence the conception of *interaction;* the feelings of one person may be considered in relation to the feelings of others, hence the conception of a configuration of emotions, or, using Redl's term, *group emotion;*[2] the idea that one member has about what member x should do under certain circumstances may be considered in relation to the ideas that other members have, hence the conception of group *norms* and (with all such ideas about all members in all circumstances) the group's *normative system;* and so on. From this viewpoint, elements on each level are conceived of as being arranged into subsystems with dynamics of their own quite apart from the dynamics within individual persons who happen to participate in and contribute to them. From this viewpoint, the general question is how the whole complex operates. The sub-systems are as follows:

1. On the level of behavior, the sub-system is *the interaction system,* which is the organization of overt action among persons over time.
2. On the level of emotion, the sub-system is *group emotion,* which is the configuration of feelings among members and of their emotional responses to events that occur.
3. On the level of norms, the sub-system is *the normative system,* which is the organized, and largely shared, ideas about what members should do and feel, about how these should be regulated, and about what sanctions should be applied when behavior does not coincide with the norms.
4. On the level of goals, the sub-system is *the technical system,* which is the set of ideas about what the group should accomplish, and the plans about how it is to be accomplished.

[2] Fritz Redl, "Group Emotion and Leadership," in A. Paul Hare, Edgar F. Borgatta, and Robert F. Bales (eds.), *Small Groups; Studies in Social Interaction* (New York: Knopf, 1955), pp. 73–75.

levels of group process: behavior and emotion

5. On the level of values, the sub-system is *the executive system*, which consists of the interpretations of what the group *is*, the ideas about what would be desirable for it to become, and ideas about how it might so become.

These five systems are empirically interrelated, for certainly our feelings are affected by what we and others do, our actions are influenced by our ideas, and our rules often change with a change in our goals. A clear understanding of this complex interdependence among the sub-systems is, however, not to be expected until the student of sociology encounters more advanced problems in the study of group dynamics. A preliminary step forward is to conceive of the sub-systems separately and to comprehend the particular, and perhaps different, principles according to which each respective system operates.

Aside from clarifying the subsequent question of interdependence among the systems, the strategy of first studying them one-by-one in their own right has certain advantages. The first is that it provides a simple basis for distinguishing between different orders of groups. Taking the total universe of social organizations, including sub-human as well as human, we may differentiate them according to the number of levels on which they operate. For example, although an ant colony displays an intricately organized interaction system, there is no evidence of emotional or symbolic process characteristic of the other levels; whereas a band of gorillas exhibits patterned interaction and differentiated emotional attachments, there is no evidence of the symbolic processes required on the levels of norms, goals, and values; and while most human groups follow some set of rules, many are not free either to choose their own goal or to decide what they might in the future become. Thus, one very general way of distinguishing social organizations is according to the levels upon which they operate.

The second advantage refers to individual members in the group. Although a group as a whole, or only some of its members, may operate upon all five levels, this does not mean that all of its members must do so. A clear example is the newcomer, for although he may quickly interact with others and immediately have an emotional impact upon them, he cannot operate effectively on the other levels until he has the opportunity of learning what the group's norms, goals, and values are. It is instructive, in fact, to use his experience as a general model for suggesting both the principles according to which the sub-systems operate, and the changes in subjective experience as one enters one sub-system after the other. Characteristically, the newcomer's progress into the group occurs in four phases: (1) entry into interaction and group emotion—what is done and what is felt; (2) entry into the normative system—what should be done and what should be felt; (3) identification with the group goal; and (4) identification with other members and with the group as a whole in what it might become.

To recap a little: after illustrating the five levels, this chapter describes processes on the first two, behavior and emotion. It considers the newcomer's orientation to the group, and the group's reaction to him during this first phase. Other levels, and the experience of the newcomer in operating on them, are considered in following chapters.

Illustration of the Five Levels

Tom, Dick, and Harry are ushered into the laboratory and asked to pretend to be an admiralty board sitting on the case of Billy Budd, a young sailor who, caught in a rage but unable to speak, struck and killed the master-at-arms, Claggert. The decision facing the court is whether Budd,

59

Melville's innocent in the story, should be hanged as the law requires, or set free.[3] Tom asks Dick what he thinks. Dick replies that Budd should be set free. To this Tom agrees, but Harry disagrees. As the discussion proceeds, Tom and Dick join forces in building a strong case against Harry, who tries to counter the points the others raise.

Within a short time the pattern of interaction among the three is clear: Tom and Dick support each other, while together they direct their negative comments toward Harry, who disagrees and presents counter-arguments. Each person's action is structured; each acts from a clear position and addresses the others as one would expect. For example, Dick expresses agreement with Tom, but directs disagreements and counter-arguments against Harry. This is his part in the interaction pattern; this is his *behavioral role*.

Presently, Harry's argument becomes so convincing (apparently) that Tom doubts his former position and, much to Dick's surprise, becomes persuaded that Budd should be hanged. Dick continues to argue against the point, though now he disagrees with both Tom and Harry, who naturally agree with each other. But even with Tom's switch, the interaction pattern is still clear. Indeed, leaving persons aside, the structure is much the same as before: two parties exchange agreements while disagreeing with a third party. Yet, since Tom has switched, Harry and Dick have exchanged positions, so that their roles have changed.

This first phase of the example illustrates three points: (1) that interaction easily becomes structured; (2) that one person's part in the over-all structure is his *behavioral role*; and (3) that behavioral roles are usually interdependent in the sense that a change in one results in involuntary changes in others. (On this latter point, it is clear that when his ally deserts him for the opposition, Dick is under pressure to be consistent and act as a defender of a minority position.)

The second phase of Dick's experience begins after the decision on Billy Budd and after a general discussion of the experience in the experiment, for then the experimenter tells Dick what has actually been going on—namely, that he alone is the naïve subject in an experiment, that Tom and Harry are assistants trained to act prearranged parts, and that the purpose of the experiment is to test the reactions of persons when they are involuntarily shifted from one to another position in an interaction structure. On hearing this, Dick's face turns red. "This," he says to himself, "changes the complexion of everything! How did I appear, weak or strong? How well did I do? Did I look good or did I look like a fool?" As these thoughts go through his mind, he realizes that he feels deep anger at having been duped.

Meanwhile, Tom and Harry's confidence over having successfully played their assigned roles now changes to embarrassment and anxiety about how Dick will respond to the deception, and the experimenter wonders what emotional impact the experience will have upon Dick. "Was the experiment," he wonders, "worth this worry and worth the feelings of guilt for having placed an innocent person on the spot?" At this point, the new configuration of feelings corresponds in part to Goffman's description of "cooling the mark out,"[4] which refers to the way professional confidence men ("con men") handle the mark (victim) after he discovers that he has been "taken." Here, Dick

[3] Louis O. Coxe and Robert Chapman, *Billy Budd, A Play in Three Acts* (Princeton: Princeton University Press, 1951).
[4] Erving Goffman, "On Cooling the Mark Out: Some Aspects of Adaptation to Failure," *Psychiatry* (1952), XV: 451–465.

levels of group process: behavior and emotion

feels like the mark and the research team members feel like con men. These are their *primordial roles*.

Notice Dick's reorientation when he learns the real purpose of the experiment. In the beginning he was induced as a naïve subject to take a particular role in a prearranged structure. At the same time, he was prevented from learning the meaning of what was really going on. As part of their job, the role-players obscured from him the "real" purpose and the "real" norms and, accordingly, kept him naïve. (This means that they admitted him to some levels but excluded him from others.) Moreover, they permitted him his own assumptions about what was going on: his assumption that persons believed the arguments they presented, that expressions of affection and distastes were manifestations of actual feelings, that Tom's change of position reflected an actual change of opinion, and so on. In short, they did not correct his natural assumption that a one-to-one relationship exists between overt manifestations and covert feelings and ideas. However, when Dick is told about the game that is being played, the complexion of everything, as he says, changes. The actual historical sequence remains the same, of course, but its meaning changes. His feelings toward the persons around him shift. He must stand back and take a new view on all that has happened, and make a reassessment about where he is. Note that Dick becomes busy on these matters simply because he has learned what the real norms in the group situation are. And as he does so, we note, he shifts to a new level of group process.

Were Dick to become a role-player himself and employ the norms he has learned, he would be entering the normative system and (depending upon his assignment) a particular *normative role*. Were he to attend project meetings where role-playing performances are evaluated, modified, and improved, he would be entering the technical system where he would perform an *instrumental role*; and finally, were he to join a review conference where the value of the project to social science is evaluated, he would be entering the executive system and be playing an *executive role*. In short, the stages through which a person advances from a naïve subject to one who is responsible for assessing the entire experiment illustrate the distinction among the five levels. His definitions of the situation and his emotional experiences alter as he moves from one level to another. His reorientation is due in part to the characteristics of the sub-system on each level. And it is to the conceptions of those sub-systems we now turn, beginning with the interaction system.

Behavior and the Interaction System

Order

Observations of patterned animal behavior, ranging from traffic control and courting rituals to pecking orders, are well known among ants,[5] bees,[6] fowl,[7] baboons,[8] gorillas,[9] and other species. Man's behavior is also patterned. Partly because we are properly trained to look beyond

[5] Wilhelm Goetsch, *The Ants* (Ann Arbor: University of Michigan Press, 1957).

[6] K. Von Frisch, *Bees, Their Vision, Chemical Senses and Language* (Ithaca, N. Y.: Cornell University Press, 1950).

[7] C. A. Murchison, *Handbook of Social Psychology* (Worcester, Mass.: Clark University Press, 1935).

[8] S. Zukerman, *The Social Life of Monkeys and Apes* (New York: Harcourt, Brace, 1932).

[9] George B. Schaller, *The Mountain Gorilla, Ecology, and Behavior* (Chicago: University of Chicago Press, 1963).

61

the surface of overt behavior in order to infer what a man means by what he says, or what he wants by what he does, we tend to overlook the design that exists on the surface of interpersonal behavior. We tend therefore to underestimate the extent to which man in general and man in groups either follows or creates an ordered, often ritualized way of interacting. This is gradually being corrected by applying systematic methods of observation like that of Bales described in Chapter Two.

With a set of categories which considers how one act is related to the next, the investigator is able to record the dynamic relations of interaction. He is able to study the dynamics of the interaction system in its own right. For example, an observer employing a set of categories labeled with letters of the alphabet records in one group the sequence *A B A B A B A B* . . . ; and in another group he records *F K T A G S L W D Q*. . . . The first is *ordered* but the second is *unordered*; he might designate the first "an *A B A B* system" and the second "a random system." Whether the *A B A B* system in question involves a witness replying to a lawyer's questions, or a vendor handing over produce in exchange for money from buyers, the observer can distinguish an ordered system from a random one. And quite apart from the nuances of the action, its causes, its subjective meaning, and its consequences, he can characterize interaction by its formal characteristics. (The question of *why* order occurs in one case but not in another can be reserved for and answered by research on the other four levels.)

Let us say that in another comparison the observer records a sequence in one group that is first *ordered*, then *disordered* (*A B A B A B F T C L K R D* . . .), while in the second group he records a sequence that is first *unordered*, then *ordered* (*D K C R L T F B A B A B A* . . .). Under what conditions, he will be led to ask, does an ordered system lose that order? Under what conditions does an unordered system gain order? What are the differences between groups that exhibit the two types of series?

To carry the observations one step further, let us say that he observes one group wherein a previous order is lost but then regained, and another group wherein a new order appears following a disruption. What are the conditions, he will be led to ask, which differentiate a group that returns to its previous pattern, from a group that shifts to a new order? Whether the first case represents an unsuccessful revolution and the second a successful one, the point is that the systematic features of the sequence of interaction can be recorded and summarized as basic data on the group. Phases from one period to another within a single group may be compared, and sequences in one group may be compared with those in other groups. Order, or lack of order, in act-by-act sequences is an elementary feature of interaction systems; methods for detecting it are relatively simple to devise, and easy to apply.

Distribution of Action among Participants

A second feature of interaction systems is the distribution of activity among members. Bales and his associates recorded the frequencies with which each member directed action toward each other member in a series of groups ranging in size from three to 10 persons. A summary of 18 six-person groups is shown in Table 2. Results were obtained by: (1) rank-ordering members in each group according to their total output; (2) constructing a matrix with both rows and columns ordered according to rank-order of output; (3) entering into matrix cells the frequencies of actions from each member so ranked to each other member (as well as to the group as a whole); then (4) adding together the 18 matrices.

levels of group process: behavior and emotion

Table 2

Aggregate Matrix for 18 Sessions of Six-Man Groups

Person Originating Act	To Individuals						Total to Individuals	To Group as a Whole 0	Total Initiated
	1	2	3	4	5	6			
1		1,238	961	545	445	317	3,506	5,661	9,167
2	1,748		443	310	175	102	2,778	1,211	3,989
3	1,371	415		305	125	69	2,285	742	3,027
4	952	310	282		83	49	1,676	676	2,352
5	662	224	144	83		28	1,141	443	1,584
6	470	126	114	65	44		819	373	1,192
Total Received	5,203	2,313	1,944	1,308	872	565	12,205	9,106	21,311

From Robert F. Bales, Fred L. Strodtbeck, Theodore M. Mills, and Mary E. Roseborough, "Channels of Communication in Small Groups," *American Sociological Review* (August 1951), XVI: 463.

Note the gradations throughout the matrix. Once members are ranked by output (and the rows ordered according to that rank), then other totals fall in order: note the column totals, the cell entries in each column, and the cell entries in each row. Also note that with few exceptions, interaction tends toward higher ranks; e.g., rank two speaks to rank one more than rank one speaks to rank two (1,748 vs. 1,238), and so on throughout the matrix. All in all, the matrix exhibits a remarkably systematic distribution. It suggests that the way group members tend to interact with one another can be stated in a set of simple principles. The suggestion would be stronger, of course, had each individual group (or a majority of them) exhibited the tendencies before being lumped together.

As a follow-through on these findings, Stephan and Mishler recorded outputs and receipts of students in 36 college discussion groups varying in size from two to 12 members.[10] They discovered that the percentage of contributions of students in a given rank-order could be adequately estimated by the following simple exponential function: $(P_i = ar^{i-1})$, where P_i is the estimated percentage for students ranked i in output, r is the ratio of any rank to the percentage for the next higher rank, and a is the estimate for students ranked highest. When applied to an estimation of receipts, the function served almost as well. (In neither case did their estimates include the instructor.) Their findings are additional evidence that tendencies in the systematic distribution of action among group members can be stated in simple, formal principles.

These observations are of tendencies and are, of course, not absolute. In fact, departures may prove to be as frequent as pure cases, if for no reason other than the influence of such factors as: (1) formal status differences among members (e.g., children in the presence of adults or guests in the presence of their host); (2) the goal of the group and the procedures required to attain the goal (e.g., a teacher instructing students, in contrast to patients reporting to their therapist; or a supervisor clarifying a new directive, in contrast to elders advising the chief); (3) sub-group formations (e.g., a split jury or a

---

[10] Frederick F. Stephan and Elliot G. Mishler, "The Distribution of Participation in Small Groups: An Exponential Approximation," *American Sociological Review* (1952), XVII: 598–608; reprinted in Hare, Borgatta, and Bales (eds.), *Small Groups*, pp. 367–379.

63

group with cliques that have their respective spokesmen); and (4) personality characteristics of members—and, of course, other factors.

Group Size

The number of persons in a group affects both the distribution and the quality of interaction. Stephan and Mishler confirmed the original observations of Bales and his associates and clarified the effects of group size when they discovered that the parameter a in the function given above changes regularly with group size. They propose that: $a_n = 234/(n + 4)$ for outputs and that: $a_n = 157/(n + 4)$ for receipts. This is to say that, leaving the teacher aside, as classes increase in size, participation becomes flatter—adjacent ranks become more alike both in output and in receipts.

Slater found the quality of action to vary with group size.[11] After using Bales' method to score 24 groups ranging from two to seven members, he devised an "index of inhibition," which consisted of the ratio of "safe" acts to impulsive, aggressive acts (Bales' categories 3, 7, 8, and 11 to categories 1, 2, 4, 10, and 12). Comparing the ratios in groups of various sizes over four discussion sessions, he found: (1) that as group size increases, the index of inhibition decreases; and (2) that as members become better acquainted through the course of the meetings, inhibition drops more for larger groups than for smaller ones. For the types of groups he observed, he suggests that as size increases, "the consequences of alienating a single member becomes less and less severe. . . ."

> In the larger group, physical freedom is restricted while psychological freedom is increased. The member has less time to talk, more points of view to integrate and adapt to, and a more elaborate structure into which he must fit. At the same time he is more free to ignore some of these viewpoints, to express his own feelings and ideas in a direct and forceful fashion, and even to withdraw from the fray without loss of face.[12]

Restricted Channels of Interaction

The above studies show that even when interaction is free and open, a systematic pattern tends to appear. Apparently there is an "economy" of interaction, an economy which is modified by a number of variables including group size. As mentioned in Chapter Three, Bavelas considered the causal chain from the other direction. Instead of asking how members tend to order and restrict their own interaction, he asked what effects a fixed or restricted pattern of interaction might have upon the group. What effects might various networks of communication have upon, let us say, satisfaction and effectiveness of the group in solving given problems? In Chapter Three we described how Bavelas and his associates experimentally established and varied the channels of communication among five members in order to test the effect of such patterns upon group efficiency and member satisfaction.[13]

In a follow-up study, Leavitt tested the effects of four patterns: the circle, ⬠; the chain, o—o—o—o—o; the wheel ⊹; and the "y," ⋋o—o.

He found that speed and accuracy in solving a problem were greater in the last two centralized networks but that, in general, satisfaction was greater in

---

[11] Philip E. Slater, "Contrasting Correlates of Group Size," Sociometry (1958), XXI: 129–139.

[12] Ibid., p. 135.

[13] See above, page 44.

levels of group process: behavior and emotion

the others.[14] Heise and Miller found that problems requiring an accumulation of information could be better solved in open networks, while problems requiring synthesis and insight could be managed more easily in the centralized ones.[15] Shaw found that persons could better distinguish relevant from irrelevant information in open networks than in others.[16]

In an interesting and important variation, Cohen and Bennis tested the effect of a change in network.[17] One set of groups worked first with the wheel, then with a completely open situation; a second set worked with an open situation on both occasions. They found that whereas the groups having first worked in the wheel tended to remain centralized rather than to shift to a more open and more gratifying network, the groups having first worked in the open network tended to keep channels open rather than to shift to the more efficient, centralized networks. Their work suggests further tests on the effects of tradition, satisfaction, and efficiency upon the voluntary establishment of networks. Meantime, the evidence clearly indicates that restricted interaction channels affect both member satisfaction (an element in group emotion) and problem-solving efficiency (an element of the technical system).

The Upshot

The few studies reported above suggest certain elementary features of the interaction system. They show both that interpersonal behavior tends to become ordered, and that situational factors affect the characteristics of that order. These are probably indications of future discoveries showing that human interaction is both highly complex and systematic. Meanwhile, however, enough is known to say that a newcomer entering a group is likely to be cast into a particular behavioral role and to play that particular part whether he and others are aware of it or not. This role is likely to affect his view of the group, what he can learn, what he can and cannot do, and how he feels about himself and about others. Changes in the system will involuntarily alter his role; and, in turn, what he does or does not do in his role, particularly as it changes, cannot help but affect the rest of the system to some extent.

Feelings and Group Emotion

In their study of adolescent groups, Sherif and Sherif reaffirm an important point about groups:

> Individuals do not form groups of their own choosing just to be, mechanically, one of a set, or because of any inherent tendency to conformity, or because they want to regulate their behavior in this or that direction. They come together and interact with strongly felt urges and with desires experienced as their own, whether these be desires to be accepted as a person in one's own right, desires to gain social distinction, sexual urges, wishes for desirable objects and instrumentalities, desires for exciting leisure-time activities, searches for recognition, or desires to prove themselves. . . . Individuals come together

14 Harold J. Leavitt, "Some Effects of Certain Communication Patterns on Group Performance," *Journal of Abnormal and Social Psychology* (1951), XLVI: 38–50.
15 G. A. Heise and G. A. Miller, "Problem Solving by Small Groups Using Various Communication Nets," *Journal of Abnormal and Social Psychology* (1951), XLVI: 327–336; reprinted in Hare, Borgatta, and Bales (eds.), *Small Groups*, pp. 353–367.
16 Mark E. Shaw, "Some Effects of Irrelevant Information upon Problem-Solving by Small Groups," *Journal of Social Psychology* (1958), XLVII: 33–37.
17 A. M. Cohen and Warren G. Bennis, "Predicting Organization in Changed Communication Networks," *Journal of Psychology* (1962), LIV: 391–416.

65

. . . and stay together because they experience *some* strong motivational basis. . . .[18]

When in the presence of others, man's needs, desires, wishes, and feelings of fear, frustration, estrangement, pleasure, affection, satisfaction, and solidarity are the ingredients of group emotion. No one ingredient exists in isolation, rather they all are in some sort of interdependent relationship. What a person in a group does makes a difference to other members; how one feels has a contagious effect upon the feelings of others; and one's needs, or signs of those needs, arouse emotional responses in others. There is perhaps constant interplay among the emotional experiences of persons in groups.

Interplay often results in a structure of emotional relations among members which can quite easily be ascertained, formulated, and confirmed, as in the following two cases described by Redl:

> There is a group of sixteen-year-old girls in a class of a girls' high school. In charge of them is a male teacher—young, attractive, but narcissistic enough so that they are not too greatly frightened sexually from the outset. It is known that in some such cases "the whole class falls in love with him." From that moment on, they will act like a group. . . . Despite their infatuation for him, it would not be surprising if the teacher complained that he had trouble with discipline—that these girls did not obey him or follow his wishes without pressure.[19]

> In a coeducational class of approximately sixteen-year-old children, there is one especially pretty girl, rather narcissistic. In similar situations one frequently finds a whole cluster of boys loving and adoring her in various ways, but equally unsuccessful insofar as their wish for exclusive possession goes. The girl is equipped with special skill for keeping them all equidistant and yet equally near. Symptoms of dense group formation may sometimes be observed among these boys. They seem very close to each other, and yet their relationship is not genuine friendship. . . . This becomes evident when the girl ultimately decides in favor of one of her suitors. The other boys then begin to hate him as their rival, with the exception perhaps of the one or two who may move even closer to the successful colleague and, thus, enjoy some of the satisfactions denied to them. . . .[20]

"There is no doubt," explains Redl, "that the teacher (in the first example) and the girl (in the second example) are playing the role of central person without whose presence this type of group formative process would not have been evolved." [21] The mechanism of group formation is: "The children choose one and the same person as an object of their love, and on the basis of this similarity they develop group emotions between each other." [22] There is no doubt, one can add, that the emotional orientations of the persons in both cases are arranged in a clear and ascertainable structure.

Bion has observed an interesting phenomenon in his therapy groups. He found that his patients interpreted the purpose of the group to be his healing them. They assumed that they had no work to do themselves, rather that he was to do it all. They were surprised and puzzled, then later angered, by his

---

[18] Muzafer Sherif and Carolyn W. Sherif, *Reference Groups, Exploration into Conformity and Deviation of Adolescents* (New York: Harper, 1964), pp. 243–244.

[19] Redl, "Group Emotion and Leadership," in Hare, Borgatta, and Bales (eds.), *Small Groups*, p. 79.

[20] *Ibid.*, pp. 79–80.

[21] *Ibid.*, p. 80.

[22] *Ibid.*

levels of group process: behavior and emotion

assumption that *they* were the ones who had to work if they were to get well. Their assumption of being dependent upon him polarized their emotions towards him, and his contrary assumption that they work to understand themselves polarized his feelings towards them. Consequently, group emotion in this case was structured around two opposite poles.[23]

Whereas both Redl and Bion suggest mechanisms according to which a group forms, Freud describes a hypothetical structure of group emotion which substantially precludes group formation. We refer to his famous description of the primal horde.[24] The value of the formulation is not its correspondence to the life of earliest man (although he seemed convinced of its plausibility, others have dismissed the formulation as a "just so" story simply because of the lack of supporting evidence relating to earliest man); instead, its value is in its correspondence to the unconscious emotional relations among members— or, in our present terms, the structure of group emotion—which is likely to exist in any small group where one person has unquestioned superior power over others. The following are highlights of Freud's formulation.

The father (and chief) is omnipotent and absolutely narcissistic. His personal wants are served without respect to others. He leads a band of impotent sons who are dependent upon him for protection yet who are deprived of all sources of gratification, including sex. The chief pre-empts all of the women for himself. He is both revered and hated by the sons. Their desire to kill him is immobilized first by the fear of retaliation in case they do not succeed, and second by the fear of being murdered by the strongest of the brothers in case they do succeed. The women (hardly mentioned by Freud) apparently respond to the masculine superiority of the chief. Fear, reverence, hatred, attraction, omnipotence, impotence, self-indulgence, total deprivation— these are the emotions which in a particular arrangement constitute the primal horde. Narcissistic omnipotence on the one hand and narcissistic impotence on the other are its central features.

The Concept of Group Emotion

As the examples above suggest, the elements of group emotion include: (1) the needs and drives which serve in the first place as causes of group formation; (2) feelings of satisfaction or frustration resulting from actual group experience; (3) interpersonal attachments and animosities; and (4) feelings of attachment to, or alienation from, the group as a whole. In general, the concept of group emotion refers to the configuration of those conscious or unconscious instinctual and emotional elements and processes occurring within and among persons which affect what the aggregate of members can and cannot do, say, believe, and think, or affect the likelihood of what is done, said, believed, and thought. If we conceive of a field of forces operating at each moment and affecting what does and does not happen in the group; and if we select those forces which originate in members' drives and feelings; and, finally, if we conceive of those particular forces together, as a differentiated and organized arrangement of forces—then that arrangement is what is meant by group emotion.

Can individual emotions be conceived of collectively? Since a group *per se* cannot think, is it not fallacious to use the notion of "group mind"? Since

[23] W. R. Bion, *Experiences in Groups, and Other Papers* (New York: Basic Books, 1959), pp. 29–34, 77–86.
[24] Sigmund Freud, *Group Psychology and the Analysis of the Ego* (New York: Liverwright, 1949), pp. 90–100; also Sigmund Freud, *Totem and Taboo* (New York: Norton, 1950), pp. 125–161.

emotions are internal, individual processes, and not group processes (in the sense that a group might "feel" something), is it not fallacious to refer to group emotion?

An analogy may help to suggest the usefulness of the notion of collective group phenomena. Consider iron filings distributed at random over a surface.[25] (By "random" is meant that if one photographed a number of scattered inch-squares on the surface and compared the distribution of filings in the various photographs, one would be unable to identify by the distribution of the filings the location of the area photographed.) Next, assume that a magnetic current is passed through the field. The filings alter their orientation and line up in some characteristic pattern. The current, as a vector passing through the field, has organized the filings. Patterns in photographs of selected areas would now reveal the location of those areas, for they are simply parts of a larger, organized field. Although the vector does not appreciably alter the individual character of each filing, it does alter the relationship among the filings. By passing first one, then another vector through the field, one may observe and compare the different types of relationships resulting from the various vectors. One may meaningfully refer to structures of relations among individual elements.

In the human situation, instinctual and emotional processes occurring within individuals correspond to the filings. Events which arouse, evoke, alter, or transform those processes are vectors corresponding to the electrical current. When such events either arrange or rearrange into a recognizable pattern the set of emotional processes among a number of group members, we may meaningfully and legitimately refer to a structure of group emotion.

Vectors and Structures of Group Emotion

Here are four examples of the structure of group emotion: (1) The presence of an outside observer usually alters the emotional state of members; they feel vulnerable and, as we saw in Chapter One, seek, perhaps unconsciously, either to incorporate or to expel him. (2) It was suggested in Chapter Two that when subjects who have been conscripted for an experiment confront one another in the laboratory, each one knows that the others are present because they were conscripted. The fact of "presence-through-conscription" is a vector, inasmuch as it organizes both feelings of deference toward the experimenter, and a sense of detachment among members. (3) In the role-playing experiment described above, Dick's flush of anger on being told he has been deceived is a vector: it increases the tension among the experimental team, and arouses feelings of guilt and self-doubt. (4) The attractiveness and narcissism of the girl in Redl's second example above is a vector: it evokes both love for her and, among those who love her, a sense of being in the same group.

Of course, some events serve as multiple vectors—for example, when a leader splits the group into two cliques: followers and rebels.

The examples we have given are of primary vectors. There are secondary ones as well. A secondary vector is a manifestation of an emotional response which, when read by members, causes an arousal of yet other feelings. Such is the case when members in a frightened group show their fear, and in so doing reveal that no one is unafraid. It is also the case when the absence of a fearless member leads first one person, then all the rest, to a panic response.

---

[25] From an example given by Paul A. Weiss in Roy R. Grinker (ed.), *Toward a Unified Theory of Human Behavior* (New York: Basic Books, 1950), pp. 117–121.

levels of group process: behavior and emotion

In other words, the act which reveals the emotional state of the group, thereby resulting in a new emotional state, is a secondary vector.

Primary and secondary vectors often combine to produce highly differentiated structures of group emotion. These structures may be conducive to group formation, as those described by Redl, or they may preclude such formative processes, as in Freud's case of the primal horde.

Formulating the Dynamics of Group Emotion

Although many persons operate effectively with an intuitive sense of interpersonal dynamics, the step from *familiarity with* to formulating an effective way of *thinking about* emotional processes is a large and difficult one. Aside from ancient and durable observations such as the function of the scapegoat and the solidifying effects of an external enemy, the more advanced attempts at formulation have been made by practitioners, clinicians, teachers, and consultants who have had the opportunity to observe a variety of long-term groups and to identify those formations and dynamic changes which tend to be common or to recur.

For example, Bion, in addition to the group's assumption of dependence upon him (mentioned above), identified three formations: (1) mobilization of group energy for either attack against a target (fight) or for an escape *en masse* from the field (flight); (2) turning to one another for intimate contact and gratification (pairing); and (3) rechanneling instinctive processes into joint work.[26] Semrad, a psychoanalyst, group therapist, and group trainer, proposes that a necessary condition for the development of a working relationship among members is that the leader enter intentionally the role of scapegoat, thereby absorbing the hostility arising from various sources, and freeing members to deal more easily with one another and with the group's task.[27] Redl has identified 10 mechanisms whereby orientation toward a central person results in group formation. One was referred to above. Others include: (1) the case when members love their leader, identify with him in their ego-ideal (what they would most like to be) and, with this in common, are then able to identify with one another—a mechanism first formulated by Freud in *Group Psychology and the Analysis of the Ego*; (2) the case when members fear their leader, identify with him in their "super-ego," become subject to joint constraint and, although together, lack comradeship; and (3) the case when members who might be overcome by guilt feelings and fear of their own drives are saved and brought together by a person who, being free of their conflicts, easily does what they dare not do.[28]

From a different viewpoint, Whitaker and Lieberman try to clarify otherwise confusing episodes in therapy groups by identifying the underlying and largely shared conflict that members are experiencing and attempting to resolve. A "focal conflict" exists, for example, when, countering the wish of each member to be specially favored by the therapist, is the fear that he will punish them for such a demand. One attempt to resolve the conflict is for members to become more alike.[29] The combination of the wish, the fear, and the mirroring of similarities constitutes one structure of group emotion.

[26] Bion, *Experiences in Groups*, pp. 77–113.

[27] Elvin Semrad, et al., "The Field of Group Psychotherapy," *International Journal of Group Psychotherapy* (1963), XIII: 452–575.

[28] Redl, "Group Emotion and Leadership," in Hare, Borgatta, and Bales (eds.), *Small Groups*, pp. 86–87.

[29] Dorothy Stock Whitaker and Morton A. Lieberman, *Psychotherapy Through the Group Process* (New York: Altherton, 1964), pp. 14–40.

Research on Group Emotion

As we indicated in Chapter One, systematic empirical research on emotional processes creates difficult technical problems. For one thing, emotional processes cannot be directly observed, but instead must be inferred from indirect manifestations. Since there are many modes through which a given feeling is made manifest, and of course similar modes reflecting different feelings, a sizable sample of episodes is required before a person is well enough understood for the observer to infer reliably his emotional state. Consequently, there is a lag between the emotional experience and its assessment—a lag that is considerable when only one person is being assessed, and so of course much greater when the experiences of all members are being considered. Indeed, as the number of persons to be understood increases, the interrelations increase at a geometric rate, and in short order the problem can become overwhelming. Finally, since group emotion is collective rather than atomistic, and systemic rather than additive, adequate assessment requires information on first, second, and third-order relationships—and this, of course, extends the lag even further. In fact, few persons (if any) have been able both to trace the course of changes in group emotion in a given group, and clearly tell others how it is done.

In spite of these difficulties, researchers have tried to assess processes related to group emotion. Mahl, for example, has attempted to devise a technique for assessing feelings of individuals; [30] Birdwhistell has "coded" body movement and gestures for what feelings they express [31] and Horwitz and Cartwright have used projective techniques to bring out latent group processes.[32] The latter technique is based on the assumption that just as dreams, interpretations of ink blots, and stories told in response to pictures provide clues to an individual's emotional processes, a group's mythology, rituals, and artistic creations, including joint stories told in response to projective pictures, provide clues about the latent emotional issues among its members. In an exploratory study they found a correspondence between the content of group stories and features of the group as estimated by other means—for example, between the frequency of hostile acts by characters in the story and freedom of expressing hostility in the group, and between positive acts by characters in the story and a sense of solidarity in the group.

Using a similar technique, Torrance asked 71 11-man bomber crews to tell joint stories about two pictures, one of a group in a working situation and the second of a group during off-hours. In comparing crews rated on effectiveness by their superiors, he found that effective crews told stories about working groups that were both more successful and more solidary, and that effective crews were more emotionally expressive in response to the informal picture, including more conflict, more friendship, more discord, and more pleasure.[33] Mills used projective pictures to estimate changes both in members' feelings toward the person in charge, and in members' emotional relationship

[30] For a discussion of this problem area and for references, see George F. Mahl and G. Schulze, "Psychological Research in the Extra Linguistic Area," in T. A. Sebeak, A. S. Hayes, and Mary C. Bateson (eds.), *Approaches to Semiotics* (London: Morton, 1964), pp. 51–124.

[31] R. L. Birdwhistell, *Introduction to Kinesics* (Louisville: University of Louisville Press, 1952).

[32] M. Horwitz and Dorwin Cartwright, "A Projective Method for the Diagnosis of Group Properties," *Human Relations* (1953), VI: 397–410.

[33] E. P. Torrance, "Perception of Group Functioning as a Predictor of Group Performance," *Journal of Social Psychology* (1955), XLII: 271–282.

70

with one another, over a six-week period.[34] And Mann, selecting the leader as a critical focal point in the structure of group emotion, has devised a method for screening every act and every statement for indications of how members orient themselves emotionally toward him.[35] These studies suggest the possibility that both the latent emotional relations among members, and the emotional orientation of the group as a whole, can be inferred from a careful analysis of the content of what is said in the group, including what is said about outside objects, events, groups, and so on.

Summary

The major points about group emotion are as follows:

1. Persons do not shed their instinctive drives, their desires, their wishes, or their feelings when they come into contact with one another; instead, their confrontation with one another is in large part in the service of those drives and feelings.

2. In the interpersonal situation, a given person's feelings rarely exist in isolation; instead, they both influence the feelings of others and are affected by the feelings of others.

3. This interplay of drives and feelings results in a more or less complex configuration (whose characteristics and consequences cannot be fully explained with reference solely to the experiences of the individual) which is designated *group emotion*.

4. A given person's part in the configuration is his *primordial role*, examples being "the person everyone loves," "the one who can heal us all," and (on the negative side) "the black sheep" and "the scapegoat."

5. Structures of group emotion differ in their effect upon group capabilities. For example, a group based upon fear and suspicion of its leader tends to be more edgy and less venturesome than one based upon respect for and trust in its leader.

6. Primordial roles differ in their effect upon individual capabilities. For example, "the darling" of the group tends to be kept just that while "the instigator" is egged-on.

7. The over-all growth of the group and its various members is affected either positively or negatively by the structure of group emotion.

8. More systematic research is required in order to advance beyond the suggestive statements about group emotion (made above), to the stage where we have a working knowledge of just how variations in the structure of group emotion affect personal and group experience.

Upshot for the Newcomer

In the beginning the newcomer characteristically finds himself adjusting to existing patterns of behavior and seeking a secure position from which to operate. He observes what others do and usually responds by doing what others call on him to do. Meanwhile, he classifies others, perhaps unconsciously, into those who are important to him and those who are not. He senses those who disturb him and might endanger him, and seeks those with whom he might be comfortable. In general, he desires those with whom he can safely find gratification. In being oriented toward the pattern and to-

---

[34] Theodore M. Mills, "Authority and Group Emotion," in Warren G. Bennis, *et al.*, *Interpersonal Dynamics* (Homewood, Ill.: Dorsey, 1964), pp. 94–108.

[35] R. D. Mann, "The Development of the Member-Leader Relationship in Self-Analytic Groups" (unpublished manuscript, University of Michigan, 1964).

ward the fulfillment of needs, he acts in the behavioral role, and experiences a primordial one.

During this first phase, his orientation is *pre*-symbolic, *pre*-cultural, and *pre*-normative. Although he follows a pattern, he is not aware of the meaning the group gives to the pattern; although he experiences emotional exchanges, he does not appreciate their significance to the group. This is because he does not yet know the ideas that exist in the minds of other members. While he may quickly detect patterns of behavior and structures of interpersonal feelings, he needs more information, and needs to employ a higher order of thought processes before he can determine how members define what is going on and how they think about it. Only when he can infer such ideas (or is told them and can accurately assess what he is told) can he learn the group's culture, know what the values are, and know what the rules and norms are. Only then can he know the meaning—the local group meaning—of what he and others do and feel. Until he is able to infer ideas about action and about feelings, and to relate those ideas to his own ideas, he remains uncertain as to what, in terms of the local culture, those acts and feelings in fact are.

The length of time a newcomer remains at the behavioral and primordial levels varies from very short for the experienced and versatile person to a number of years for the infant, and to forever for members of the sub-human species such as baboons, gorillas, and so on. As indicated above, although such sub-human groups are ordered and organized, they are apparently incapable of using symbols and, therefore, are incapable of having an idea or of inferring an idea about how life *should* be ordered and organized. This means that they are unable to advance from the behavioral and the primordial levels to the normative level or to the other levels. In our discussion, we assume that the newcomer *is* able to symbolize, and consequently to advance to other levels.

levels of group process: behavior and emotion

levels
of group process:
norms and goals
five

In their study of adolescent groups in the southwestern region of the United States, Sherif and Sherif find that although a boy may be a skillful basketball player, he will not become a *bona fide* member of the gang unless he learns: (1) that he should never criticize a fellow's performance while in competition; (2) that while in competition "it is O.K. for him to foul if he can get away with it" but that (3) it is not O.K. when practicing with fellow members (though he will find that the leader has a right to foul more frequently than do others).[1] He must learn many other rules, including: (4) that stealing is permissible providing one uses common sense in not getting caught, that one has a clear plan, that one does not have too many persons involved, and that one takes other reasonable precautions; (5) that going with a new girl is permissible so long as it is announced to the group in case there are any objections; (6) that one does not trespass upon another's right to a girl while he is exercising that right; and, most important (7) that one must protect the integrity of the group. The newcomer will be told truthfully that some boys have been expelled from the group because they "ratted" to parents or to the police, and others because they deserted the gang in a street fight. Thus, the prospective member learns that there are rules he must not violate if he is to be accepted in the group, and that he must demonstrate an ability to learn and to know rules, and to govern himself

[1] Muzafer Sherif and Carolyn W. Sherif, *Reference Groups, Exploration into Conformity and Deviation of Adolescents* (New York: Harper, 1964), pp. 164–183, 269–273.

73

according to them. In general, it is through his response to group codes that the newcomer signifies his desire to be a full-fledged member.

Norms and Normative Control

The Concept of Group Norms

Rarely can rules be inferred directly from behavior; they are ideas rather than patterns of behavior, and so must be learned as ideas. This fact is discovered by newcomers through typical object lessons. For example, the young child finds that he is prohibited from doing what he sees others in the family doing; that what was rewarded in the past is now punished; that what is permitted on one occasion is prohibited on another; that there is not a general one-to-one correspondence between the type of acts he and others perform, and rewards and punishments. The new gang member's object lesson is similar when he discovers that while his fouling in practice offends the group, the leader's fouling does not. The obvious inference is that fouling has various meanings and that the principle that applies to him is not the same as the principle that applies to the leader. Still, in other instances, when he observes that some acts (such as "ratting") are disapproved of no matter who commits them, the obvious inference is that this principle applies to everyone equally. Thus, through experience he learns that the significance of an act is not in the act itself but in the *meaning* the group gives it. And he learns that this meaning may alter according to who commits it, and the circumstances under which it is committed. Fortunately for the student of sociology, though this variability in the meanings given to behavior is confusing to the newcomer, it is quite simply accounted for through the sociological concept of *group norms*.

Group norms are ideas in the minds of members about what should and should not be done by a specific member under specified circumstances.[2] Referring to the example above, a shared idea among members is that no one should foul a fellow member during practice, but that because of his position, the leader has a special privilege in this regard. It is a shared idea that one does not trespass on another's right to a girl, though if there is to be an exception, it would be made for the leader. Finally, it is a shared idea that new members and the youngest members be given the disagreeable tasks. Because norms are ideas and are therefore subject to elaborate qualifications, they can specify the many fine distinctions necessary to accommodate different persons, times, occasions, and circumstances.

Classification of Norms

Norms, which have all too often been thought of as haphazard or random standards, actually help orient persons to each other, providing guidelines as to how certain universal interpersonal issues are to be managed by the parties in question. Parsons presents a classification of these issues and of the possible answers.[3] Norms in any society or group, he suggests, must provide answers to questions relating to at least four issues: (1) Are relations among members to be based upon the expression of the feelings they have toward one another, or upon the assumption that those feelings are to be suppressed and controlled (*i.e.*, is group emotion to have precedence over normative control, or vice-versa)? (2) Is involvement with one another to be total and

[2] George C. Homans, *The Human Group* (New York: Harcourt, Brace, 1950), pp. 121–127.

[3] Talcott Parsons and Edward A. Shils (eds.), *Toward a General Theory of Action* (Cambridge: Harvard Univ. Press, 1951), pp. 80–88. Parsons has subsequently dropped the self-collectivity dilemma. Consequently, we list the four remaining ones.

levels of group process: norms and goals

unbounded (as with parent and child), or is it to be restricted and spec
with driving instructor and pupil)? (3) Is the significance of the othe
due to the unique relation one has with him (as brother, cousin, or frie... ,,
is it to be due to the fact that he represents a type, or a class, of person (a
servant, a client, or an employer)? (4) Is the significance of the other to be due
to his qualities (steady and wise), or is it to be due to how he performs (as a
scientist, as an athlete, and so on)?

The norms across groups may be compared by reference to the answers
their members give to these questions. Although various combinations of answers are possible, some are more likely than others, and with two combinations
an easy contrast can be made between the traditional primary group and more
technical groups—for example, between the family (where relations are based
upon expression of feelings, unbounded involvement, unique ties, and personal
qualities) and the surgical team (where relations are based upon suppression of
emotions, restricted involvement, technical qualifications, and skill in performing the prescribed tasks).

Parsons' classification is useful for comparing different groups because it
may be applied to all members alike in a given group, and may therefore be
used to characterize the group as a whole. Another type of classification is
helpful for analyzing the differences in privileges and obligations among members within the same group: Hohfeld's classification of bilateral legal relations
is an example; though designed for more formal legal systems, the scheme has
been applied to primitive societies by Hoebel, and is appropriate for small
groups as well.[4] Briefly put, the four basic normative relations are as follows:
First, person A has a *demand-right* while person B has a *duty*, meaning that
according to the law (norms), A has a right to expect that B do (or refrain
from doing) x for him, while B has a duty to do (or refrain from doing) x for A.
Example: gang member John has a right to his girl without interference from
other members; the other members have a duty not to interfere. Second, person
A has a *privilege-right* while person B has *no demand-right*, meaning that A can
do x without being subject to B's penalty, and that B has no redress if A does x.
Example: John may sell his car to anyone he chooses without becoming subject
to disapproval from another member, Pete, while Pete has no redress when
John sells his car to whomever he wants. Third, person A has *power* while B
is *liable*, meaning that A may voluntarily create new duties for B, and new
demand-rights for himself. Example: in response to gang leader Harry's request
for volunteers to do a special job, Pete offers. Harry may or may not accept
Pete as a volunteer—that is his power; but if he does accept, Pete cannot
renege—that is his liability. Fourth, A is *immune* while B has *no power*, meaning
that A is not obligated to accept a new relation proposed by B, while B has no
power to create the relation if A chooses not to do so. Example: in response to
John's proposal that henceforth gang decisions be made by majority vote, the
leader, Harry, announces that the question will be discussed later. Harry is
free to accept or reject John's proposal; John has no power if Harry happens
not to accept the proposal.

Norms vary in the ease with which they can be learned. Some (such as
statements in bylaws and code books) are codified; some are easily recognized
and verbalized by members; others are less explicit and become apparent only
when they are violated; still others are unconscious, as in the case of some taboos
which are in themselves unthinkable ideas. Whether easily learned or not, group

[4] E. Adamson Hoebel, *The Law of Primitive Man, A Study in Comparative Legal
Dynamics* (Cambridge: Harvard University Press, 1954), pp. 46–63.

levels of group process: norms and goals

norms are a set of statements about feelings and behavior. They are cognitive and moral statements which screen, evaluate, prescribe, and proscribe feelings and actions. As statements they are distinct from feelings and from behavior. They exist in symbolic form in the mind, and are elements of group culture. Their dynamics are cultural rather than emotional and behavioral, and it is for this reason that they are considered to be on a distinct level differentiated from the levels of behavior and emotion.

Deviance

In gangs reported by Sherif and Sherif, it is deviant to criticize a fellow player during competition; it is deviant to go with a new girl without clearance; it is deviant to "rat" to the police; and it is deviant to leave during a fight. The formal sociological concept is simple: An act is deviant when it violates a shared idea about what, on the occasion in question, should or should not be done.[5]

Of course, behavior may in some circumstances depart from tradition without being deviant. For instance, although a passive member may become highly active, such a change is not in itself deviant; it would be deviant only when the norms prescribed that he remain passive. Also, taking an unpopular position on an issue is not deviant unless there is a norm prescribing that all hold similar opinions. Correspondingly, although altering one's feelings toward another constitutes a change in group emotion, such a change is not deviant unless there exists a norm prescribing the former emotional relationship. Deviance, to repeat, refers to the formal relationship of action in violation of the norms.

Sanctions

Sanctions are acts in response to other acts. They carry at least two messages, either or both of which may be explicit or implicit. The first message refers to the relation of another act to the norms (such as, "What you have done was what should have been done," or "That act goes against the rules"). The second is a demand about future relations between actions and norms, either to reinforce a previous relation ("We should like to have you do more of what you have done") or to alter a previous relation ("You must cease and desist"). In the latter case, what must be changed in order to achieve conformity varies from altering a discrete act to altering the total relation of the member of the group. For example, negative statements may vary greatly in range, thus: (a) "You are accepted but that type of act is inappropriate"; (b) "Not only is that act unacceptable, but your attitude is wrong"; (c) "Your action, your attitude, and your relation to the group are all inappropriate"; (d) "Your membership in the group is to be terminated"; (e) "Your life is to be terminated." Of course, like all other actions, sanctions are themselves subject to norms, whether they be based on an accurate assessment of those norms, or an erroneous assessment. And they may be legal or illegal, legitimate or non-legitimate—and, therefore, either conforming or deviant.

The Normative System

In larger societies the law of the land, and the judicial system, are familiar as explicit and formal parts of the normative system. Other

[5] For a discussion of the concept of deviance, see Albert K. Cohen, "The Study of Social Disorganization and Deviant Behavior," in Robert K. Merton, Leonard Broom, and Leonard S. Cottrell, Jr., (eds.), *Sociology Today, Problems and Prospects* (New York: Basic Books, 1959), pp. 461–484.

levels of group process: norms and goals

components are less familiar. Although many societies and most small groups neither codify all their laws nor formalize all their judicial procedures, they nonetheless regulate their expression of feelings, and their interaction with reference to a more or less complex set of ideas about what should and should not be done. This set is designated *the normative system*. As a concept, the normative system refers to more than norms; it refers in addition to ideas about how norms themselves should be maintained, reinforced, and even changed. For instance, to assess the normative system of a group, one abstracts from the total group culture the following overlapping sets of ideas: (1) the norms; (2) by implication, the definitions of deviance; (3) the order of importance of the various norms; (4) by implication, the seriousness of deviant acts; (5) the boundaries of the norms (defining what is of group concern and what is of private concern, defining, in Hohfeld's terms, areas of immunity and no-demand right); and (6) the arrangement according to which norms, sanctions, and the boundaries of the normative system itself are to be legitimately altered. Altogether, the normative system refers to how social control *should* be exercised in the group. How control processes actually operate—in particular, whether they conform to or depart from stipulations in the normative system—is a question to be answered by empirical investigation.

Dynamics of Normative Control

How norms evolve, how they are learned and maintained, how they influence persons and events and, in turn, how they are modified by circumstances, are central problems in the sociology of groups.[6] The following sample of hypotheses and propositions only suggests the range of interest and viewpoints of those concerned with such questions. In 1951, Festinger and Thibaut hypothesized that the more cohesive the group (that is, the greater the total set of forces upon members to remain in the group), the greater the group pressures upon members to conform to the group norms.[7] A corollary is that the greater the attraction to the group, the greater the pressure to conform. Although Festinger cites evidence from a field study and a number of laboratory experiments to support the hypothesis, there remains a question of how cohesive groups in these studies actually were, and of whether factors in the situation other than cohesion might have contributed to observed differences in confromity.[8]

More recently, Walker and Heyns have argued that even if group pressure is greater in cohesive groups, such pressure alone would not be enough to cause a change in behavior toward the group norms.[9] A change depends specifically upon whether, for the person in question, conformity is a means of reducing personal needs. When need reduction is contingent upon conformity, then persons modify their behavior and attitudes. It is under these conditions that

---

[6] For a current review of research on deviance and social control in groups, see A. Paul Hare, "Interpersonal Relations in the Small Group," in Robert E. L. Faris (ed.), *Handbook of Modern Sociology* (Chicago: Rand-McNally, 1964), pp. 217–271, especially pp. 217–226. This chapter also contains an excellent bibliography on small groups research.

[7] Leon Festinger and John Thibaut, "Interpersonal Communication in Small Groups," *Journal of Abnormal and Social Psychology* (1951), XLVI: 92–99.

[8] Leon Festinger, "Informal Social Communication," in Leon Festinger, *et al.*, *Theory and Experiment in Social Communication* (Ann Arbor: Research Center for Group Dynamics, University of Michigan, May, 1950), pp. 3–16; also see reprint in Dorwin Cartwright and Alvin Zander (eds.), *Group Dynamics*, 2nd ed. (Evanston: Row, Peterson, 1960), pp. 286–299.

[9] Edward L. Walker and Roger W. Heyns, *An Anatomy for Conformity* (Englewood Cliffs, N. J.: Prentice-Hall, 1962).

77

"the stronger the need, the greater the tendency to conform" applies. Thus, if in a gang confidence is placed only in those who demonstrate their unconditional commitment to the gang by conforming, then the more a boy wants to belong, the more likely he is to alter his thought and style to coincide with the norms. "For social pressure to be effective in producing conformity," Walker and Heyns suggest, "the person must see conformity as an effective avenue to achieving the goal of acceptance of the group." [10]

In an intricately designed experiment which has been replicated by Emerson,[11] Schachter tested the hypothesis that when a member in a cohesive group deviates, others will first actively try to convert him to the norms and then, if they fail to do so, will reject him. He further suggests that both tendencies (to change and to reject him) are stronger as the group is more cohesive.[12] A paraphrase of this position is that tightly-knit groups tend to be less tolerant of deviance than loosely-knit ones.

In following Cohen's admonition that conformity and deviance be considered as two facets of the more general process of normative control,[13] Dentler and Erikson have considered the functions that deviance serves for the group. Contrary to the layman's general assumption that deviance is bad and something we should have less of, their interesting conclusion is that deviance serves a positive function for the group.[14] First, since norms, as ideas in the minds of members, are often implicit and are rarely entirely obvious, the appearance of deviance (as an overt demonstration of what should not be done) makes the norms more explicit, thereby helping members to become more articulate about them. Instances of what should not be done clarify ideas about what should be done. Second, the group's emotional and behavioral reaction to deviance helps members apprehend what their group is and is not. For instance, to feel offended by an act and to see others similarly offended provides information about oneself and about the group, information that perhaps could be gained in no other way.

> Comparisons which deviance makes possible help establish the range in which the group operates, the extent of its jurisdiction over behavior, the variety of styles it contains . . . [which] are among the essential dimensions which give a group identity and distinctiveness. . . . A group is distinguished in part by the norms it creates for handling deviance and by the forms of deviance it is able to absorb and contain.[15]

For these and related reasons, Dentler and Erikson suggest that groups "will resist any trend toward alienation [total rejection] of a member whose behavior is deviant." [16]

To Dentler and Erikson's point can be added the argument that the exercise of legitimate sanctions is more than equilibrating. Rather than simply restoring a previous state, it increases group solidarity in two ways. First, for those who feel inclined to deviate but check themselves from doing so, public

---

[10] *Ibid.*, p. 96.

[11] R. M. Emerson, "Deviation and Rejection: An Experimental Replication," *American Sociological Review* (1954), XIX: 688–693.

[12] Stanley Schachter, "Deviation, Rejection and Communication," *Journal of Abnormal and Social Psychology* (1951), XLVI: 190–207, reprinted in Cartwright and Zander (eds.), *Group Dynamics*, 2nd ed., pp. 260–285.

[13] Cohen, "The Study of Social Disorganization and Deviant Behavior," in Merton, Broom, and Cottrell (eds.), *Sociology Today*, pp. 461–484.

[14] Robert A. Dentler and Kai T. Erikson, "The Functions of Deviance in Groups," *Social Problems* (1959), VII: 98–107.

[15] *Ibid.*, p. 101.

[16] *Ibid.*, p. 102.

levels of group process: norms and goals

sanctioning of the actual deviant not only justifies their self-control, but affirms the fact that the norms back of self-control coincide with the norms back of group control. Consequently, the affinity of person with group is reinforced. Second, the overt sanction is an undeniable demonstration that members care enough about the norms (and the group) to act on their behalf and to attempt to maintain them. Consequently, commitment to the norms is both demonstrated and reinforced.[17]

The Normative Role

The distinction between behavioral, primordial, and normative roles is that the first refers to action, the second to feelings, and the third to ideas about actions and feelings. For example (and as we have seen), how one responds to a command of a parent is an element of one's behavioral role; and how one feels about oneself and one's parent while responding in such a manner is an element of one's primordial role. The element of the normative role is the idea that in these circumstances a child should obey his parent. *The normative role* is comprised of the total set of ideas which, for a person in a particular position in the group, stipulate how he should (and should not) behave toward others, and how he should (and should not) express his feelings toward them. In addition, it includes ideas about how he should control himself, how he should control others and, in general, how he should act in order to maintain the normative system.

While a person can perform behavioral and primordial roles by reading and responding to signals (that is, by observing and fitting into a pattern, or by redirecting one's response to avoid pain), one must be able to deal with symbols and with ideas to perform in the normative role. One must be able to formulate and to convey, to receive and to transmit ideas about, what is happening. One must be able to converse about what is being done, and to deal with messages about messages. For example, "What you said (a message) is x and not y (a message about a message)." This level of thought corresponds to the level of communication referred to by Reusch as *meta-communication*, or communication about communication.[18] For instance: "What I said was x; what I meant to say was x + 1." "What I said was x, but I was only kidding. Don't take it seriously." "By the way you state your agreement, I gather that you actually disagree. Am I right?" When a person thinks to himself on this level, he arrives at private meanings about what is said and done; when group members openly discuss matters on this level, they arrive at public meanings about group processes. Past events are reviewed, defined, evaluated, and reinterpreted. Lessons are learned, and new rules are often formulated.

Through communicating about communication, the newcomer acquires a new perspective on his group experience. For one thing, he is better able to conceive of what is going on, while still participating in the process. For another, his view of the group norms change. In the beginning, group rules are interpreted as both absolute and as constraints upon personal freedom. However, through talking over with others both what has been going on and what should have been going on, and, in particular, through taking part in changing the rules, the newcomer perceives them as less absolute and more flexible. They appear man-made and mutable. In addition, they appear as guidelines as well as con-

---

[17] For a discussion on the source and consequences of sanctions, see Emile Durkheim, *The Division of Labor in Society*, trans. George Simpson (New York: The Free Press of Glencoe, 1933), pp. 70–100.

[18] Jurgen Ruesch, *Therapeutic Communication* (New York: Norton, 1961), pp. 423–436.

straints. The newcomer becomes better able to conceive of norms as statements of the acceptable limits within which he is free to operate; he becomes less interested in what is prohibited and more interested in what is permitted. When he learns what is allowed, then he gains both a sense of assurance and a greater latitude in his behavior. Thus, through experience on the meta-communication level, the newcomer benefits from one of the positive functions of norms—namely, a conceptual vantage-point from which to interpret what is happening, and upon which to base his own choices of behavior.

Group Goals and Their Accomplishment

Personal Goals and Group Goals

If a goal is a mental construct, how can a group, which has no mind, have a goal? F. H. Allport, an early social psychologist, would say that it cannot; to him the idea would be another example of the group fallacy. He argues that:

> . . . alike in crowd excitements, collective uniformities and organized groups, the only psychological elements discoverable are in the behavior and consciousness of the specific persons involved. All theories which partake of the group fallacy have the unfortunate consequence of diverting attention from the true locus of cause and effect, namely, the behavioral mechanism of the individual. . . . If we take care of the individuals, psychologically speaking, the groups will be found to take care of themselves.[19]

Sociologists would argue to the contrary: first, that groups as systems cannot be explained solely through knowledge of their constituent parts, and second that the classical position stated by Allport arises from a confusion between personal and group elements. An example will clarify the distinction between personal and group goals and suggest the utility of, and the necessity for, collective concepts.

Consider competitive games in general, and chess in particular. Each chess player plays to win—to win is the personal goal of each—and thus the goals of the two players are similar. Now, although the fact that both parties have similar personal goals is an interesting feature of this dyad (that is, of this particular pairing of two parties), it provides no information about the nature of their collective goal. It would be fallacious, for example, to conclude that since both parties aim to win, "to win" is the goal of the group: similar personal goals do not make a group goal.

To infer the group goal we must first conceive of the dyad as a unit (that is, we must think of the two parties as one party, group, unit, or whatever) and then ask what present or future state *of this unit* is thought by the parties to be desirable. Clearly, that state cannot be "to win," for the dyad as a unit is not a contestant and has no opponent; the dyad itself can neither win nor lose. Consequently, to refer to the goal of the unit as "winning" is meaningless. Do we conclude from this that the concept of a group goal is meaningless? On the contrary, there is an idea in the minds of the two parties which refers to a desirable state of the dyad: it is to have a high-quality contest which each party wants to win, wherein play is imaginative, in which superior play does win. The group goal, as distinct from personal goals, then, is to have a good contest. The sociologist uses the concept of group goal because it helps explain

[19] Floyd H. Allport, *Social Psychology* (Boston: Houghton Mifflin, 1924), p. 9.

levels of group process: norms and goals

phenomena that cannot be explained by personal goals, whether taken alone or in aggregate. For one thing, the rules of the game of chess are not devised primarily to supply a winner (though, of course, they provide for one); rather they are artfully constructed in order to create an absorbing and interesting contest. If we imagine the origin and development of the game of chess, we can see that the making of the rules is a means toward the end of a good game. For another thing, opponents are selected, or chosen by each other, not to assure that one party wins over the other, but rather to assure that the contestants are well matched. Thus the matching of players is another means toward the end of a good game.

Our suggestion is that the student conceive of two levels of goals in any formal contest, the first referring to the occasion as a whole and the second referring to the individual participants. The goal toward which all parties cooperate is to achieve a high quality contest, while the goal of the individual contestant is to win. Clearly, the two are interdependent, for the game must be well-designed to stimulate good play and participants must be motivated to make the game a good one. Still, the relationship between the two goals can be more clearly specified for there is an expectation that the party who enters the role of contestant will play to win. This is to say that the norms of the occasion demand that the individual contestant accept as his personal goal the desire to win, or at least that he play as though this were his goal. Otherwise, the overall goal of a good contest cannot be achieved. Sociologically speaking, the game norms demand certain personal goals: to play with no intention of winning is not only deviant in a formal sense but lets one's opponent down and tends to undermine the contest. Many contestants know, on the one hand, what little pleasure is derived from winning against opponents who do not care but on the other hand the satisfaction gained when, in a tight contest and in spite of excellent play on their own part, they lose. Clearly, satisfaction depends upon more than achieving one's personal goal of winning. So we see that setting up the rules of play, the process of selecting contestants and the conditions which provide satisfaction are examples of group phenomena which cannot be accounted for by personal goals but which are easily explained when we conceive of the goal of the occasion, or of the group as a whole.

Two points need emphasis. First, the group goal is not the simple sum of personal goals, nor can it be directly inferred from them. It refers to a desirable state for the group, not simply to a desirable state for individuals. As we have seen, the personal goal in chess is to win *over* one's opponent, while the group goal is to have a good game *with* one's opponent. The second point is that the mental construct of the group goal resides not in some mystical collective mind, but in the minds of group members. It cannot meaningfully exist anywhere else. It exists there along with other mental processes including personal needs, personal wishes, and personal goals. It may be shared by most or all members, but since many other ideas are shared, that is not its distinction. What sets the concept of group goal apart is that in content and in substance it refers to the group as a unit—specifically, to a desirable state of that unit. The concept resides in the minds of individuals; the referent of the concept is the group as a whole. There is no contradiction here, and there is no fallacy.

The Instrumental Role and the Technical System

In his *Two Years Before the Mast,* Dana describes a scene aboard the ship *Pilgrim* as it sets sail from Boston's lower harbor.[20] As a

---

[20] Richard Henry Dana, *Two Years Before the Mast* (New York: Bantam Books, 1963).

new and wholly inexperienced hand, Dana stands to the side, out of the way, and is at some loss in giving his account. He does not understand the language of the officers, nor the relationship between the mate's orders and the men's reactions, nor how the men's movements change the positions of the booms, spars, rigging, and sails. "There is not so hopeless and pitiable an object in the world," he writes, "as a landsman beginning a sailor's life." [21] Still, he shares the excitement as the ship catches the wind and moves out. Weeks later, when again the *Pilgrim* sets sail, the scene is similar except for Dana, who this time moves quickly in response to an order, and carries out his assignment. He knows what to do and how to do it, and takes pride in doing it well. In the interim, Dana has come to know the men and has learned the language and the ways of life aboard a merchant ship, and he feels at home. He has learned what has to be done in order to get a ship under way, and precisely how his particular assignment fits in with those of others so that together they accomplish the task. In sociological terms he has learned, and is operating in, an *instrumental role*.

In general, a person enters the *instrumental role* in a group when he (1) conceives of the group goal, (2) accepts it, (3) commits his personal resources, intelligence, skill, and energy toward accomplishing it, and (4) gives its accomplishment higher priority than his own goals, the group's norms, and the existing pattern of emotional relationships among members, including his own popularity and personal comfort. He is committed to the goal and prepared to act on its behalf. He evaluates both his own performance and the performance of others more in terms of *effectiveness* than according to conformity to rules. Men aboard ship judge each other on many grounds, but the judgment of a sailor is on seamanship.

For the officers and crew leaving Boston on the *Pilgrim*, the immediate *group goal* was to get the ship under way. Their *technical system* was comprised of: (1) their "know-how" in handling the ship and in coordinating the essential activities among the men; (2) their standards for assessing the *effectiveness* of any one activity in contributing to getting the ship under way; and (3) their standards for judging the total operation as a success or a failure. Dana's *instrumental role* is his specific assignment, plus the standards of effectiveness he and others applied to what he did in carrying it out. He had a target and was guided primarily by the standards defining what was and was not effective in reaching that target. He was primarily responsible for upholding standards of superior performance and for assuming his share of responsibility for actually reaching the target, and this responsibility took precedence over maintaining the norms.

Research on Group Effectiveness

The most consistent (and perhaps the most obvious) empirical research finding in our area of discussion is that a group whose members know what to do in order to reach their target is more likely to approach it than a group whose members do not have the "know-how." The same is true for a group under a skillful and experienced leader (when compared with one under an inept and inexperienced head). Technical know-how is especially important when the goal is external—that is, when it involves a change in the environment (such as building a bridge) or a change in relation to the environment (such as finding one's way in strange territory). More interesting sociologically is the question of which factors account for differences in effectiveness among groups who are more or less equal in technical knowledge and skill. One such factor is the incentive system, otherwise known as the arrangement of rewards for performance. In a classical laboratory experiment, Deutsch demonstrated the differences between a cooperative arrangement and a competitive one.[22] He broke up a university class into 10 five-person groups which were to meet for a three-hour problem-solving session each week over a five-week period. Their participation substituted for class work. He divided the groups into two sets: cooperative and competitive. In the first set the ratings, which were to be counted in the course grade, were based on the total performance of the five-man team, and all members were to receive the same rating. In the second, ratings were based upon the comparison of one team member against another, with the possibility that the better the performance of one member, the lower the ratings of others. A battery of measures, including a record of interaction, observers' ratings, and group members' reports, showed substantial differences between the two sets of groups. In the cooperative arrangement, members (1) were more concerned about completing their problems, (2) exchanged more ideas and reported less difficulty in communicating with each other, (3) coordinated their activity through dividing functions and pooling results, (4) expressed positive feelings among one another more frequently, and (5) showed (according to observers' ratings) clearer insight and better judgment in deciding their next steps. They also solved puzzles faster, and were superior in assessing human-relations problems that were presented to them. In all these respects, groups in the cooperative arrangement addressed themselves to the situation and managed their internal relations in a way superior to groups in the competitive arrangement.

It should be noted that in spite of this, when the productivity of separate individuals is considered, no significant difference in the two arrangements was found. But even so, evidence from the study shows that when the way to reach one's *individual* goal is through working with others in order to accomplish the *group* goal, then group effectiveness is superior to groups wherein rewards are granted individuals irrespective of team performance. In the first case, accomplishing the group goal is a means toward individual goals, while in the second, personal goals are given priority over group ones.

A second factor is group cohesion—the degree to which members feel emotionally close to one another and share an emotional attachment to the group. Some studies show that cohesive groups are more productive than less cohesive ones. For example, Berkowitz found that in the absence of an outside superior, cohesive groups produced more than less cohesive ones.[23] Other studies show that effective groups tend to be cohesive. It is found, for example, that bomber crews which received superior ratings tended to associate with each other more frequently during off-duty hours than crews which received lower ratings.[24] Evidence in these and other studies suggest a general circular relation between effectiveness and group solidarity. Demonstrated competence seems to draw members closer together, while being close together seems to increase the likelihood of successful group performance. This circularity may be broken when group members are strongly committed to an important group goal. Never-

22 Morton Deutsch, "An Experimental Study of the Effects of Cooperation and Competition Upon Group Process," *Human Relations* (1949), II: 129–152, 199–231.
23 L. Berkowitz, "Group Standards, Cohesiveness and Productivity," *Human Relations* (1954), VII: 509–519.
24 L. Berkowitz, "Group Norms among Bomber Crews: Patterns of Perceived Crew Attitudes, 'Actual' Crew Attitudes, and Crew Liking Related to Aircrew Effectiveness in Far Eastern Combat," *Sociometry* (1956), XIX: 141–153.

theless, under these circumstances, the effective group remains so even though its members do not become intimate, the case in point being bomber crews which felt beyond all else that they had critical missions to accomplish.[25] Another factor affecting group productivity is the "fit" or, as the case may be, the "clash" between the personalities of its members. Schutz suggests that while some persons are most comfortable when they are close to their associates, others find such closeness disconcerting; that while some persons want to follow another's lead, others resent anyone in authority; and that while some want to lead, others are content to work along with those who lead.[26] Groups may be composed in such a way that these basic interpersonal orientations are either compatible or incompatible. When they are compatible, Schutz suggests, the group should be more productive than when they are incompatible. Schutz tested this hypothesis in a carefully designed experiment on 12 college-student groups meeting for 14 sessions over a six-week period. He found that both the groups composed of those who were comfortable when close, and the groups composed of those who wanted to keep their distance, were in general more productive on a series of tasks than were the groups which were mixed—*i.e.*, wherein some wanted to be close while others wanted to keep their distance. The "clash of personalities" which appears to have interfered with group effectiveness was between those who wanted to be close and those who did not want to be close.

Other studies suggest factors that impair group effectiveness. Rosenthal and Cofer [27] found that the presence of a person who displayed disinterest and distaste for the task at hand undermined the entire group effort, or at least contributed to low productivity. In a study of 72 governmental and industrial conferences, Fouriezos, Hatt, and Guetzkow rated comments on the extent to which they expressed self-oriented needs of the speaker, and found that where the frequency was high, not only were members dissatisfied over procedures and decisions, but interpersonal conflict was high and fewer decisions were actually made.[28] These studies show that the presence of those who are committed to ends other than the group goal tends to undermine the effectiveness of the group as a whole. To these factors which impair group productivity can be added the frequently observed practice of workers banding together and establishing a group norm to restrict output.[29] The basic factor in these cases is, of course, the conflict between the goal of the workers and the goal of management.

Consequences of Technical Success

In pursuing and accomplishing a goal, groups do not remain unchanged; rather they gain information, experience, and confidence. The technical system changes through the acquisition of new information, new techniques, new standards of evaluation, and so on. Group emotion changes through the deeper commitment of members to the group and to each other.

[25] *Ibid.*

[26] William C. Schutz, *FIRO: A Three-Dimensional Theory of Interpersonal Behavior* (New York: Rinehart, 1958).

[27] D. Rosenthal and C. N. Cofer, "The Effect on Group Performance of an Indifferent and Neglectful Attitude Shown by One Group Member," *Journal of Experimental Psychology* (1948), XXXVIII: 568–577.

[28] N. T. Fouriezos, M. L. Hatt, and Harold Guetzkow, "Measurement of Self-Oriented Needs in Discussion Groups," *Journal of Abnormal and Social Psychology* (1950), XLV: 682–690.

[29] F. J. Rothlisberger and W. J. Dickson, *Management and the Worker: Technical vs. Social Organization in an Industrial Plant* (Cambridge: Harvard University Press, 1939), pp. 524–548.

levels of group process: norms and goals

And these changes permit greater flexibility in coordinating activities for a more effective performance. Empirical research shows that when more successful groups are compared with less successful ones, members in the more successful ones tend: (1) to commit themselves more fully to the group goal; (2) to communicate with each other more freely and more clearly; (3) to coordinate their activities more closely; and (4) to feel more friendly toward one another. For instance, Berkowitz and Levy found that during a break in problem-solving, bomber crews which were doing well on the problems continued discussion about the tasks and raised their aspiration level for the next ones, while less effective crews avoided talk about the tasks and actually lowered their aspiration level.[30] Shelley found that members in successful groups take a more favorable attitude toward their groups than do those in less successful ones.[31]

Returning to Deutsch's experiment on cooperation and competition: his results may be interpreted from the viewpoint of the consequences of success. It is reasonable to assume that over a five-week period, superior performance and higher productivity are themselves causal factors, inspiring enthusiasm, easing communication, creating friendliness, and allowing closer coordination. The various changes probably have reciprocal effects upon each other, or even a spiral effect whereby success increases both the amount of energy available for pursuing the goal and the information and skill in reaching it, while in turn, new energies and new social and technical skills increase the likelihood of success. This spiral relation may prove to be one of the more important principles of group dynamics.

The Newcomer and the Four Levels of Group Process

The newcomer rarely enters into all areas of group life at once. Nor does he progress from a novice to a fully responsible member by a smooth and gradual process. Instead—and perhaps like the parts played by man from infancy to old age—he enters the group by distinct steps, often marked by abrupt changes in behavior, in feelings, and in ways of perceiving others and in relating to them. (Such was the case of Dick in the role-playing experiment described in Chapter Four.) These abrupt changes are important to the sociologist, for they signify the existence of distinctly different vantage points from which members orient themselves toward the group. Differences in these vantage points are due, in part, to the existence of distinct levels of group process: as one moves from one level to the other, one's vantage point and, consequently, one's entire perspective changes.

We have suggested that the newcomer characteristically enters the group through four stages. During the first stage he operates within the behavioral and the primordial roles which are oriented respectively toward the existing interaction pattern and toward drives and their gratification. During the second he adds a new role, the normative, which is oriented toward what should be done and what sorts of feelings should be expressed; this role alters the way he acts and how he expresses his feelings. During the third stage he adds still another role, the instrumental, which is oriented toward what the group as a unit should accomplish and which again alters his previous roles, since that accomplishment implicates actions, feelings, and norms. The fourth stage, of entering the executive role, is discussed in the next chapter.

[30] L. Berkowitz and B. Levy, "Pride in Group Performance and Group-Task Motivation," *Journal of Abnormal and Social Psychology* (1956), LIII: 300–306.
[31] H. P. Shelley, "Level of Aspiration Phenomena in Small Groups," *Journal of Social Psychology* (1954), XL: 149–164.

New Demands

As the newcomer accumulates a repertoire of roles on additional levels, new demands are made upon him and new capabilities are required of him. In order to shift to the normative level, he must not only be capable of understanding the ideas about what should and should not be done, but he must also be capable of exercising control over himself and others. In his normative role, then, he must both comprehend and participate in the normative control over group process. This means that he must operate according to a more complex feedback process than is required in the earlier stage. Steps in the new feedback process are as follows: given an act by some member, (1) does the act correspond to the group's ideas about what the act should have been? (2) if it does, then no response is necessary and attention is directed to other matters; (3) if, on the other hand, it does not correspond, then what sanctions are to be applied? (4) of the possible sanctions, which ones are, in terms of the norms, legitimate? (5) applying the sanction; (6) assessing the response to the sanctions, i.e., reading its effectiveness in inducing the actor to conform to the norms; (7) altering the sanction to increase the likelihood that subsequent behavior will conform to the norms. In short, he assesses all that occurs in terms of the norms, and assumes responsibility for maintaining the norms.

Still other demands are made on the newcomer as he enters the instrumental role. He must be able to subordinate personal goals to the collective goal. He must be capable of conceiving the relation between the group as a whole and its environment. In addition, he must employ a still more difficult feedback process: given the group goal as a target and an act on the part of a member, (1) what (aside from the normative considerations above) are the act's consequences for moving the group toward the target? (2) when the act is judged effective, then how is it to be reinforced? (3) when the act is judged ineffective, then what can be done to improve its effectiveness? (4) acting in order to improve effectiveness; (5) assessing this attempt to improve effectiveness; and (6) altering both the ways of trying to reach the goal and one's attempts to influence the performance of others. One of the more difficult steps in the feedback process on this level is to read, moment by moment, the indicators of effectiveness. Since what is done usually has multiple effects, it is seldom obvious what the more significant ones are; and since goals are often more efficiently reached by indirect means, it is seldom clear whether a current direction is the best one. These difficulties are compounded when both the group and its environment are constantly changing. In this respect alone, assessments on the instrumental level require more information and are more demanding than assessments on the normative level, where, as we have seen, the comparable question is how behavior corresponds to the norms.

New Latitude

It is interesting to note that as the newcomer becomes more fully committed to the group's culture, including its norms and goals, he becomes less constrained by the demands of the group structure as it currently exists. This is because he becomes committed to what *should be* done rather than to what *is being* done, and to what *might be* accomplished rather than to what *is being* accomplished. Let us take the shift from the behavioral to the normative role to explain the point.

As indicated above, one of the positive functions of social norms is that they provide general guidelines to behavior. Before a newcomer learns the norms, he can only adjust his actions according to directly observed patterns of

86

behavior. In these circumstances, his behavior is immediately contingent upon what someone else does. Consequently, the newcomer expends energy, being constantly on the alert and remaining prepared to alter instantaneously his response according to someone else's next move. His dependence is illustrated by the young gorilla who must stop foraging and move elsewhere when the older gorilla chooses to move. The young gorilla's behavior is entirely contingent upon the behavior of the older one. The newcomer's uncertainty is illustrated by the substitute football player who does not know the plays, or a new musician who has no score, or a new actor who has no script. To play at all would require great skill, flexibility, and training. The pressure is relieved, of course, when the plays are known, the score is available, and the script is memorized.

Just as the football player adjusts his moves according to the design of the play, the musician according to the design of the score, and the actor according to the design of the drama, the person entering the normative role adjusts his behavior according to the design of his relationship to the group. That design is given by the norms. As guidelines, they replace his dependence upon moment-to-moment observations of what others do. As guidelines, they free him from the immediate demands of the existing interaction pattern. Instead of following others, he is free to follow the norms.

New latitude is again gained in the shift into the instrumental role. With a clear collective goal to be accomplished, the question of effectiveness takes precedence over the question of conformity. Often the most effective course of action calls for a change both in traditional modes of behavior and in past norms. As a consequence, the norms are less binding. Moreover, deviance is not automatically sanctioned. Instead, it is first assessed from the viewpoint of the group goal, for it may be effective, even though deviant, and therefore may be reinforced rather than punished. With the instrumental perspective, norms become less absolute, and the range of possible behavior widens.

However, with new latitude in the instrumental role comes a new risk; namely, the possibility of failure and of having that failure measured. In this sense the newcomer becomes more vulnerable as he gains latitude. By the same token, he has an opportunity for being effective and, therefore, of becoming more valuable to the group. The fact that the stakes are higher is another indication that he is operating on a new level of group process.

executive
processes
six

This chapter describes the executive role—one entered by those who assume unrestricted responsibility for the group and aim to increase its capabilities.[1] The executive functions, as implied in Chapters Three and Four, are to develop group consciousness and to influence what the group is to become. These functions not only require more skill than the other roles we have discussed but, as we shall explain, place the executive in an unresolvable conflict. Ultimately, consciousness of the human group demands knowledge of all causes and effects of all events or, relative to our present knowledge, omniscience; and, ultimately, determination of group character and history means the power to reconstitute persons and social organizations at will or, relative to most of us, omnipotence. Pragmatically, the executive cannot know all, or do all. Consequently, he must select from among the universe of causes and effects those which are relevant and important; and he must choose among courses of action for those which are strategic. For this reason the next chapter presents in broad outline a sociological paradigm which, in combining the structural-functional and cybernetic features discussed in Chapter One, points to a limited number of issues of strategic importance to the

[1] For an analysis of executive functions within more formal organizations, see Chester I. Barnard, *The Functions of the Executive* (Cambridge: Harvard University Press, 1948), pp. 139–284; and W. E. Henry, "The Psychodynamics of the Executive Role," in W. L. Warner and N. H. Martin (eds.), *Industrial Man* (New York: Harper, 1959), pp. 24–33.

executive. We call them critical issues. The paradigm is meant to serve as a model. That is, if the executive applying it is true to his role, he will want to become conscious of the way he is applying it, and of its strengths and weaknesses, and to reformulate it where necessary. Executive and paradigm work together; the paradigm helps the executive learn his role and, as he does so, he feeds that learning back into an improved paradigm. But to appreciate why he needs a paradigm, it will be well for us to understand more fully the demands of his role.

The Executive Role

The first of four features of the executive's role is that his responsibility is not for parts, sectors, sub-systems, or selected levels, but for the total dynamic configuration of whole persons in an organized group within a changing environment. He identifies with this totality (which we call the *meta-group*) much as a parent identifies with his family in its life situation, or a head of government with his nation in its historical situation. The meta-group is not a single thing but a set of phenomena, all important in group experience: it includes routines of interaction; pervasive feelings such as trust or mistrust, confidence or anxiety, elation or sadness; a configuration of interpersonal and intergroup attachments and animosities; a set of written and unwritten, conscious and unconscious rules and taboos; a system of implicit and explicit beliefs and values; and so on. It has a history, current potentials, environmental demands to be met, and choices to be made. It is both a set of processes within persons, and a web of affiliations and influences extending to other persons, groups, and societies. The executive's concern diffuses throughout this multi-leveled, differentiated, polycentric, interdependent configuration.

Second, while being identified with this meta-group, the executive acts at any moment to influence what the meta-group is to become. Now, what a meta-group becomes is shaped by sequences of discrete responses to momentary situations. For example, a group that pays tribute to a more powerful one becomes a subordinate group; one that persists in its habitual ways in spite of radical environmental changes becomes a rigid group; one that waits for, and always follows, the orders of the experimenter becomes an automaton; one that cannot discard unrealistic fears becomes paralyzed; and, of course, one that pursues a self-destructive plan perishes. Groups pick their way through a career of responses to momentary situations from which they emerge with their qualities and characteristics. It is to this career that the executive directs his interventions.

A parenthetical note: the extent to which momentary responses are determined by, or are explicable in terms of, universal laws is an open question in current sociology. What is less in doubt is: (1) that choices are affected by the way members approach the momentary situation; (2) that approaches, or orientations, differ; and (3) that, consequently, laws about choices will vary from one set of orientations to another. For example, when all members are oriented to the moment in terms of a pre-established pattern of action (instinctual or otherwise), the law will be of one order, but when members are chiefly interested in achieving a highly desired objective regardless of what has happened in the past, they will be of another order. They will be of still another order (and perhaps quite difficult to formulate) when each member and the set of them collectively confront the situation as executives, conscious of the moment, of their responsibility in respect to making choices, and of the possible effects of one alternative against another. In short, laws governing momentary responses are likely to differ according to the operation or non-operation of role-systems in the group. The implication for sociology is that more complex or more viable theoretical models are required when numbers are in the more advanced roles, such as the executive, than otherwise; and the implication for the executive is that in making his own choices he cannot rely upon a simple set of formulae, or upon the ones used in less inclusive roles.

Third, the member entering the executive role decommits himself from the other roles. This process is familiar, for it occurs at each stage as the newcomer advances through the behavioral, primordial, normative, and instrumental roles. However, a review of the difference in commitment of these roles will help clarify the executive role. Whereas in the instrumental role one is committed to the group goal, in the executive role one evaluates alternative goals and, if appropriate, attempts to change the current one. Whereas in the normative role one is committed to the maintenance of the group's rules, in the executive role one is concerned with who sets the rules, how they are set and, if necessary, how their legislation might be modified. Whereas in the primordial role one is committed to the expression and fulfillment of feelings and needs, in the executive role one is concerned with how those feelings, expressed or suppressed, present possibilities for, or place limits upon, what the group as a whole can understand about itself and what it can do. In short, the executive assumes responsibility for what the group might become and decommits himself from what it has been.

Fourth, the executive is both an *insider* and an *outsider*. His stance vis-à-vis the group is comparable to the stance of the ego vis-à-vis the personality: the ego manages forces both from within and from without, and must maintain this dual orientation if it is not to collapse.

The executive—having libidinal ties, being morally obligated to others and sharing ideas and goals with them—is an insider. Yet, in his role he steps back, "becomes stranger to the familiar," and asks, as an outsider might: "What is this group?" "Who are these people?" "What is their (our) purpose?" "What are they (we) doing (becoming)?" Such questions connote detachment, distance, and estrangement—the more so to those who need the protection of the group and the security of its *status quo*. They arouse feelings of confusion, defense, and resentment toward the executive ordinarily reserved (as we saw in Chapter Two) for the outside observer. Consequently, in his dual stance the executive can expect to be the object of mixed feelings and, often, to be alone.

In summary, the executive identifies with the meta-group. He is committed not to sub-parts but to its entirety, both as it is and is becoming. He intervenes in its history and as a consequence influences its qualities and characteristics. He experiences, observes, and assesses the realities of the momentary situation. He acts and assesses the consequences of his action upon the group's capability of coping with immediate demands and future exigencies. Although he takes into account the interaction system, group emotion, the normative system, and group beliefs, values, and goals, he operates independently of these parts. He may confirm or break the routine; he may reinforce or modify the structure of group emotion; he may conform to or deviate from the norms; he may adhere to or contradict the group's beliefs and assumptions; and he may pursue or change the group's goal. As both insider and outsider, then, his commitment is to effect the meta-group as it is in the process of becoming.

90

Entry into the Executive Role

As in the case of other roles, entry into the executive role is defined by an emotional, moral, intellectual, and behavioral reorientation rather than by formal assignment, an election, or their equivalent. One may be elected to an office where one *should* operate as an executive but does not in fact do so; and one may, even without office, perform executive functions. And, since most members know something of the nature of their group and influence it by what they do, the line marking entry into and departure from the role is often indistinct. The following example, wherein the leader intentionally leaves a vacuum for members to fill, is chosen to make the point of entry clear.

Twelve senior military men gather at an east coast university for a week's seminar on executive management. Though some know each other, most do not. All have come directly from active duty, where each has a number of men under his command. They know of this seminar as "unusual," "valuable," "off-beat," "something to be experienced to be believed," "an emotional upheaval," "wild compared to the military—wild!" Most have guessed correctly that their selection to attend reflects their superiors' confidence in them. Yet, they feel they are being tested.

After signing orders and handling routine matters, and as the group settles down in its soundproof, electronically-rigged room surrounded by one-way observation mirrors, the officer in charge from Washington announces: "Many of you have heard of this seminar. As you know, we have the week here together; the schedule of the daily sessions was sent to you. And you have the reading material and the eight cases. Some of the cases are from the military, some from industry, and others are from the family, school, and so on. They all involve important problems in understanding what people do and why they act as they do. They have been studied by your predecessors in this seminar in one way or the other, as they chose. We have the material before us and we have the time together. What we do with them is up to us—entirely up to us. I have no plan, no agenda, no program for you to follow. The seminar is yours. What do you want to do with it?"

Silence follows. Several cigarettes are lighted. Chairs are pushed back away from the table. A notebook is opened and closed, then opened and closed again. The silence lengthens and still no one speaks. A heavy-set officer moves to open a window. At the end of the table another stares at the pencil he is threading through his fingers. All seem embarrassed until one member finally notes that he doesn't have a plan either, but thought all the cases were pretty good and would like to talk about one everyone has read, such as the *Semper Fi* case.

"Which one was that?"

"*Semper Fi.*"

With no more than a nod from his fellows, he begins reading from the case.

The silence proves to be an important moment for the seminar. In the simple act of throwing the seminar open to the participants, the leader shatters their expectations, and they respond with shocked silence. He breaks military custom: no orders, no specified routine, no clear ground rules, no unambiguous authority structure. Contrary to tradition, the officer in charge is handing over to others the prerogatives and duties of superior authority. Few arrangements in military society cover this contingency, and none of the guides in the rule book. In giving the seminar to the participants, the leader disavows their normal roles and provides no goal, ground rules, principles, program, or pattern as guidelines. Instead, all these must be formed by the group. In "giving" the seminar to the participants, the leader invites them to undertake responsibility for the executive role.

"The silence," one officer remarked later, "made the week. It was a shock to me. I sat there not knowing what to do. I waited for someone else to step in. No one did. I wondered if he [the leader] really meant that it was up to us or whether this was some sort of experiment. Should I take him seriously? He said it was our seminar. Does this mean he is not going to lead off? That we must decide what to do? How can we do that? We don't know how to run a seminar? I don't know these other fellows. I don't know what they want. They seem nervous, too. One thing we can do—we can make fools of ourselves. We can stick our necks out and then get them chopped off. 'Never volunteer—never volunteer'—this went through my head. It's a trap.

" 'Yet,' I thought, 'suppose he means it. We are away from the base, from Washington, from the military. We are at a university.' It may not make much sense, but I decided he meant it. I decided he thought we could do it. I felt, 'This is it—like being shoved into cold water to sink or swim.' Down deep I felt good. I was ready to give it a try. Then before I knew it, someone was reading this case, *Semper Fi*."

The officer is describing entry into the executive role: the transition from passive-dependence upon habit, tradition, rules, and someone else to select the target, to a willingness "to enter the confusion and see if anything at all can be done to salvage (create) the seminar." Later he will be heard to say such things as "I notice that when we talk about people in the cases, we are really talking about ourselves—it's as though our discussion is all in dream-talk, really referring to us when the words are about others"; "when we come close to one another we start joking as though we don't want to get too close"; "we are all acting, putting on a show, because we are afraid the Washington office is out there observing us." This officer probably does not recall that as he entered the executive role he pulled his chair up to the table, placed his pipe carefully in the ash tray, and began rapidly to scan the group to find out what was going on.

Not all of his colleagues followed him into the role. In fact, on the last day, one persisted in trying to get the group to accept a standard order of procedure governing their discussion.

The Executive System

Note an important point in the example: that being in charge and being in the executive role are not one and the same, as subordinates often imagine them to be. The role refers to an orientation to the situation and the performance of certain functions, not to a position or an office such as chairman, chief, commander, or president. In line with this, note that although the officer from Washington invites others to join him in the executive role, he does not by this act relinquish his leadership. Others may perform executive functions without taking over his position. The same is true in the teacher-student relationship when the student acquires the teacher's methods of thinking, without becoming the teacher. The distinction between position and process is shown again in the example by the fact that the invitation is (correctly) open to all and by the fact that the acceptance by one member does not preclude (it even encourages) acceptance by others. This is because executive processes are sharable, not exclusive. There is no reason inherent in the processes themselves why all members of a group cannot (a)

executive processes

assume total responsibility for the group, (b) develop self-consciousness, and (c) participate in the determination of the group's process of becoming. For this reason, it is useful to conceive of an *executive system; i.e.,* the set of all executive orientations and processes as they are distributed and organized among and performed by group members. Any member, regardless of position or office, who performs executive functions (such as contribution to the group's awareness of itself) participates in the executive system; and, any act (regardless of whether it is habitual or unique for the initiator) that performs an executive function is part of the executive system.

The executive system is the group's center for assessment of itself and its situations, for arrangement and rearrangement of its internal and external relations, for decision-making and 'for learning, and for "learning how to learn" through acting and assessing the consequences of action. As such, its purview extends like an umbrella over the other role-systems we have described. The executive system monitors behavior, emotion, norms, beliefs, goals, and their collective organization. They are contained within its orientation, but not it within theirs. They are subject to rearrangement by the executive system, but not it by them. The executive system is a partly independent, autonomous center where information about the role-systems and about the meta-group as a whole is processed and whence come both ideas about what it should become and acts designed to make it so. It holds this supraordinate relation to the other role-systems because executive processes employ a higher order of feedback process (consciousness) than do goal-seeking, normative control, and so on.

In summary: the executive system is the set of executive orientations and processes, howsoever they are distributed among members.

The Executive Function of Consciousness

It is simple enough to say, as we did in Chapter One, that consciousness—the product of third-order feedback—is a system's awareness of itself. But, more specifically, what is there to be conscious *of,* and by what method is it achieved?

Let us take an extreme position by saying that one needs to become aware of all factors and forces (elements) which affect what is and is not possible, or likely and not likely, to occur in the group. In attempting to understand the dynamics of personality, and more precisely why a given person does what he does in a given concrete moment in time, Lewin employed the concept of *field.*[2] The *momentary field* is comprised of any element, and all elements in combination, which exert an active influence (a push, a pull, a block, a detour, and so on) upon what a person does or does not do. The field is a momentary, cross-sectional view of the multiple causes of a bit of human behavior. Lewin argued that comprehension of this field makes all human action understandable and, consequently, lawful. Behavior, he suggested, is a lawful function of the interplay among elements of the field, or, according to his formula: $B = f (P \cdot E)$ where B is behavior, P is the personality of the actor, and E is the environment. $(P \cdot E)$ is the field.

We may apply Lewin's concept of the field and his formula to groups, providing we make appropriate modifications. The group field—or, as we chose to call it, the *momentary situation*—is comprised of all factors, circumstances,

2 Kurt Lewin, A *Dynamic Theory of Personality,* trans. D. K. Adams and K. E. Zener (New York: McGraw-Hill, 1935), pp. 66–80; and Kurt Lewin, *Principles of Topological Psychology* (New York: McGraw-Hill, 1936), pp. 30–40.

and forces (elements), whatever their nature or location, which have a determinant effect upon what events do or do not occur, or are likely or not likely to occur, in the group. His formula is modified to read $E_g = f (P \cdot G \cdot C)$—or, translated: a given group event is a function of the interplay among elements in personalities, the group, and the group's context. For example, the observed silence (E_g) in the military seminar described above was a function of (a) the emotional, mental, and internal control processes of each of the 13 persons present (P); (b) the previous, shared conceptions of what the seminar was to be, expectations about how its leader would act, shared feelings of surprise and frustration, the pervasive need for someone to lead, anticipated consequences of a poor show, traditional pressures against volunteering, and so on (G); and (c) the one-way mirrors, the microphone, the observer behind the mirrors, the atmosphere of freedom at the university, the ghost-like presence of superiors in Washington, as well as the present and anticipated state of the nation (C). Were one to know all the factors at play during the silence one would, for that moment, approach consciousness of the group; and were that knowledge shared by the participants, they would approach group consciousness.

Table 3 presents a further breakdown of the principal terms in the formula. The basis of the breakdown (which is the one we have used heretofore for the group; namely behavior, feelings, norms, other aspects of culture, and executive processes) is extended to personality and contextual relations in order to indicate corresponding elements in those other systems.[3] Yet the chief purpose of the table is to emphasize three points: (1) that the universe of possible causal elements spreads far beyond the physical and organizational boundaries of the group itself and, at the same time, penetrates into the deeper recesses of personalities; (2) that *any* combination or sub-set of elements within the universe of elements may comprise the momentary situation associated with a given event; and (3) that since events are themselves elements, and therefore possible causes of changes in other elements, the configuration and location of elements in the momentary situation changes from one instant to the other. The complications of this for understanding what is going on are enormous. They are so great, in fact, that social scientists have subdivided the universe of elements into sub-areas, selecting one or another for specialized study while assuming heuristically that other elements are constant. The psychologist, for instance, selects the personality sector, the social psychologist the interplay between personality and group, the sociologist the group sector, and so on. Such a division of labor is a necessary expedient in the making of a science, but it is not available, feasible, nor advisable for the executive who operates within the total complexity of a given moment in time. He is not free to select some sectors and ignore others, but must be prepared to learn about them all. This is to say that not only is the universe of elements he needs to become aware of extensive, but *no naturalistic nor A PRIORI grounds exist for excluding sectors of elements*—none, that is, if he is to contribute to group consciousness.

We may imagine consciousness as an aim, but by what method is it

---

[3] For a discussion of the relation between elements in personality and elements in the group or the social system in general, see Talcott Parsons, "The Superego and The Theory of Social Systems," in Talcott Parsons, Robert F. Bales, Edward A. Shils, *Working Papers in The Theory of Action* (New York: The Free Press of Glencoe, 1953), pp. 13–29; for an analysis of ego functions, see Anna Freud, *The Ego and The Mechanisms of Defense*, trans. Cecil Baines (New York: International Universities Press, Inc., 1946); and Erik H. Erikson, *Childhood and Society* (New York: Norton, 1950), pp. 163–234.

executive processes

Table 3

Classification of Elements in the Momentary Situation

PERSONALITY	GROUP	CONTEXT
Behavior Traits How person tends to act and interact under given circumstances.	**Interaction System** The pattern of interpersonal behavior among members.	**Physical and Social Contacts** Environmental resources and limits; the pattern of contacts with outside persons, groups, and societies.
Personal Needs and Feelings The structure of physical and psychic needs and affective processes, and the conscious or unconscious processes associated with them.	**Group Emotion** The distribution of emotional states, and the structure of affective relations among members (conscious and unconscious).	**Emotional Relations** The distribution of libidinal attractions, enmities, and alienations between the group (and its members) and outsiders, including the member's nation and other societies.
Internalized Norms The set of conscious and unconscious ideas about how one should feel, and what one should do.	**Normative System** The set of shared ideas (conscious and unconscious) about how persons, as group members, should feel, and what they should do under given circumstances; ideas about what the interaction system and group emotion should be.	**Contractual (or "treaty") Relations** The set of reciprocal obligations and privileges between the group as a unit, and outside bodies.
Beliefs and Values Explicit and implicit definitions of the world, and of preferences among alternative objects, ideas, and states of affairs.	**Group Culture (in addition to norms)** The set of shared (explicit or implicit) definitions of reality; preferences among objects, ideas, and states of affairs; and standard procedures for pursuing the desirable—all as collectively defined.	**Cultural Interchange** Definitions and evaluations of one another by group members and outsiders; the content of information, ideas, ways of learning, etc., exchanged between group and outsiders.
The Ego The person's capabilities for assessing realities and for rearranging his habits, feelings, norms, beliefs, and goals according to new circumstances and to new purposes.	**The Executive System** The group's capabilities for developing consciousness, for rearranging itself, and for altering its goals according to new circumstances and to new purposes.	**The Inter-Group Executive System** The capabilities of the group, together with outsiders, to assess, negotiate, and renegotiate their contacts, emotional relations, obligations, exchange, and, in general, their degree of interdependence.

achieved? The answer is by direct empirical observation of "all" that goes on in the group. At least this is the first of four steps.

1. *Observation.* The executive observes overt behavior, listens with "a third ear" as it were, and remembers what he sees and hears. Behavior may

be as global as the silence of the military seminar or as finite as a glance of the eye or a movement of the forefinger.

2. *Decoding information carried by behavior.* Any event, we have suggested, is caused by a combination of multiple elements. We now assume that each causal element has altered the nature of the event in the sense that without the element the event would be different. This effect is a trace of the element and as such contains information about the elements. The trace contains a message. Events, being multiply-caused, carry multiple messages which to the observer are scrambled together.

In Chapter One we referred to the analogy of the prism. We now refer to the modulators on a telephone line, an analogy used by Wiener.[4] At one end a large number of conversations are collected, encoded, then sent through a trunk line to the other end, where a modulator separates and decodes them before delivery to recipients. Were one to tap into the trunk line, one would simply hear a jumble of noises; yet, these noises could be traces of the original conversations. It is only with a modulator which "understands" the encoding procedure that sense can be made out of the noises. To the executive-observer, the original conversations correspond to elements in the momentary situation, the jumble of noises to the observable event, while the modulator corresponds to his thought processes in interpreting causal elements. Causal elements encode events; events carry multiple messages and the executive-observer decodes the messages, thereby arriving at information about the momentary situation.

3. *Inferring.* Repeating this process over a series of events and using the classification in Table 3, the executive-observer draws inferences as answers to these questions: What do these messages tell me about the personalities of persons in the group? What do they tell about the operation of the group's role-systems? What do they tell about the relation of the group to its context?

4. *Formulating.* The executive-observer arranges his inferences into a conception of the structure of, and the interplay among, elements which affect group events. He may test his ideas by intervening and judging by reactions whether or not his conception is adequate and, in time, formulate his notions as to what the group is and how it operates. As he conveys these formulations to others, feeding them in to the group's culture, he contributes to group self-consciousness.

Note that each new event may bring new information and that there is no set number of messages events carry. Consequently, *there are no A PRIORI grounds for attending to one event while ignoring another, or for knowing how many messages a given event will contain.*

The First Executive Dilemma

Our argument is that any element in the universe of elements may be causal and that any event, and any one of the many messages contained in an event, may be informative. On the face of it all are significant, none are insignificant. There are no naturalistic, or *a priori*, grounds according to which the executive can, by screening or by exclusion, simplify his task. In other words, the ultimate demands of gaining group consciousness are for omniscience. However, as suggested above, realistic limitations prevent the executive from achieving omniscience, and place him in a dilemma.

[4] Norbert Wiener, *The Human Use of Human Beings* (Boston: Houghton Mifflin, 1950), pp. 4–7.

executive processes

For one thing, the sheer volume of messages produced in the normal course of group interaction appears greater than participants can process. Although we have no accurate estimate of this volume, its scale is suggested by Pettinger and others (who wrote a sizable book analyzing the first five minutes of a psychiatric interview, and at that were highly selective of the facets they took into account [5]), and by the fact that few observers who have used tape-recordings and slow-motion cameras would claim that a still more refined breakdown of analysis would not add new (and perhaps important) information. The more angles taken on interaction, and the more minute its dissection, the more the information found. It would be easy to reduce this matter to the absurd, but the important lesson for the executive is the realization that even the most astute observers of human behavior are, relative to the amount produced, inefficient information processors, catching and decoding only a small portion of the total.

Even with improved efficiency, the executive faces another limitation to omniscience: active personal and collective resistance to self- and group awareness. Everyone has unconscious needs and wishes which he is not prepared to acknowledge and against which he constructs defenses. And each person evolves a private view of himself and the world composed in part of fantasy or illusion which, for his own comfort and esteem, he keeps secret, implicit, unformulated, and therefore beyond test. Each person, that is, has a vested, and partly unconscious, interest in preventing causal elements within him from becoming known. The same is true for the group as a collective unit. Members are subject to common unconscious needs, assumptions, prohibitions, and so on, which serve defensive functions for the group, and may serve them best by being unknown. For example, groups with a taboo against harming the leader often have a secondary taboo against acknowledging the first one, for to recognize the rule to protect him would be to admit the existence of wishes to harm him (which wishes are themselves taboo). In the family, incest is not only taboo, but talk about it is unthinkable, for it would acknowledge just those libidinal forces against which the taboo is aimed. And among the Navaho, to know about witches is a sure sign that one is a witch. The general point is that the sense of collective security is supported by unconscious and implicit agreements to keep certain feelings, assumptions, beliefs, and taboos *unrecognized*. Members cooperate, inadvertently or otherwise, to keep these elements out of awareness—to keep them, in the face of inquiry, secret. Add to this the likelihood that the executive himself is both subject to unconscious needs and wishes, and emotionally and culturally bound to the group with which he identifies, and one realizes the subtlety and strength of resistances to group consciousness.

The first dilemma of the executive who aims to increase group capabilities is that, on the one hand, he needs to know what the group is and what it can become, while on the other, because of both the volume of information and the built-in resistances to self-awareness, he cannot know all that persons are, all that the group is, nor at any moment, all that is happening. In short, the demands of his role are impossible to fulfill. This distinguishes the role from the others previously discussed: behavioral patterns can be followed, feelings can be expressed and many needs fulfilled, norms can be maintained and reasonable goals can be reached, but *consciousness of the human group, by its very nature, cannot be fully realized*. Awareness of this condition introduces

[5] Robert E. Pettinger, *et al.*, *The First Five Minutes* (Ithaca, N. Y.: Paul Martineau, 1960).

another demand of the role: namely, an attitude of humility—which is to say, the combination of a receptivity to new information (even though the past is not understood) with a readiness to revise past assessments (even though the revisions will be incomplete).[6] And, awareness of this condition means a shift from the imperative of omniscience to the imperative of selection. Pragmatically, the executive must select and screen information, must infer and formulate according to some frame of reference which purports to distinguish the relevant and important from the irrelevant and insignificant. The paradigm in the next chapter is one such guide. However, before going to it, let us consider briefly the executive's second dilemma.

The Second Executive Dilemma

Whereas the first is over *knowing*, the second dilemma is over *doing*. And while the first is common to the outside sociologist and the executive alike because both are observers, the second involves just the executive because he alone operates from within the group and is responsible for acting upon the situation when necessary. As an actor *in* the situation, the executive assumes an orientation similar to an experimenter; that is, he asks such questions as: "If act *x* occurs, what effect will it have upon group characteristic *y*?" and "If we alter part *A* of the system, what effect will that have upon part *B*, or upon the total system?" Actions become significant as causal factors, as well as sources of information. Group process is seen as interplay between elements in the momentary situation, and overt events: a set of elements causes an event and the event changes the original set of elements; this in turn causes a different event—and so on. The second dilemma is that even though his assessment might indicate what in the group should be changed (what the group could be were he omnipotent), certain basic properties of persons, groups, and the context—as he may have discovered through assessing the situation—are impervious to the will of him who wishes to change them. For instance, through what action can one person modify at will the basic needs of another—needs such as hunger, thirst, sex, security? Or alter the emotional states of anxiety, fear, antagonism, love, mistrust? Or neutralize internal prohibitions? Or supplant basic assumptions of the nature of reality? Parents, teachers, friends, and physicians are familiar with limitations in this regard. Persons and groups have integrities of their own. Through what action can one alter the nature of a group—a group, for instance, that thinks it is superior to all others, or one that believes it can be rescued only through a messiah, or one that assumes that its cohesion depends upon physical attack against an enemy, or one whose superstitions preoccupy it, or one that is coalesced through common guilt? Prophets and poets and statesmen are all too well acquainted with the difficulties in reforming such collective phenomena.

When, through experimental attempts to determine the history of the group, the executive becomes aware of those elements which are beyond his power either to modify or to create, then he confronts another demand of his role: that he be imaginative, as well as humble. He needs to devise interventions which, though small in themselves, have disproportionately large consequences upon the system; and for these he needs more than a superficial understanding of group dynamics. He needs a model which guides him to causes rather than to symptoms, and suggests what is feasible to do as well as what would be ideal to do.

[6] Karl Deutsch, *The Nerves of Government* (New York: The Free Press of Glencoe, 1963), pp. 229–233.

executive processes

Responses to the Dilemmas

The dualities of the executive role that we have mentioned, such as monitoring the group from "outside" while operating from within, and identifying with its over-all development while being oriented to the immediate situation, test the skill and balance of the group member. Even more severe, we are arguing, are his basic dilemmas of being responsible for enlightenment and self-determination, when neither is completely possible. Together these dilemmas pose a conflict to which executives respond in one way or the other—a response which has a critical effect upon their groups.

Some would-be executives escape the conflict altogether by anticipating it and by refusing to enter the role, preferring to remain in more specialized roles or in ones lower on the pyramid of responsibility. Others, especially in crises but at other times as well, call on outside help such as aid from the physician, the clergyman, the psychiatrist, the lawyer, the management consultant, the diviner, the shaman, and so on as the case might be. These responses are more straightforward than still another type, which warrant special mention because, while they appear to be solutions, particularly to members who employ them unconsciously, they are not. Four such pseudo-solutions which may appear concretely in families and in the classroom, as well as in business, industry, and government, are as follows:

1. *Intrusion and Manipulation.* Unwilling to acknowledge the realistic limitations to total information and to absolute control, the member aggressively attacks those limitations. He first (and perhaps unknowingly) seduces the group away from its original purpose and into a program of collective self-revelation where ordinary realms of privacy are invaded, persons are psychologically denuded, experiments are conducted to reveal the true nature of the group and the more sacred ideas, and symbols and relations, one after the other, are unveiled; then he uses the new "confidential" information to more effectively manipulate the group into being the sort he can control. Such a totalitarian program is justified morally by dicta like "know thyself," "to make conscious is to cure," "public confession is personal purification," and so on. Uncovering the secret and the sacred creates a sense of omniscience, and, when using knowledge of the other against him, a sense of omnipotence. To the extent of the seduction's success, the group becomes perverted into the service of the "executive," rather than being served by him.

2. *Obstructionism.* Sensitive to the dangers of a wrong move, the member inadvertently uses data from his extensive, careful observations, and ideas from his elaborate and refined analysis, as a block to action. Information and formulation are means for obscuring the situation, jamming the decision-making process, postponing clear-cut decisions, and forestalling commitment to a single course of action. And this mode of obstruction is justified by the beliefs that people and groups are infinitely complex and that though they may be comprehended at a distance, one can do more harm by acting on, or with, them than by allowing the natural processes to unfold. (Justification gains intellectual support from the organismic group model outlined in Chapter One.)

3. *Simplification and Suppression.* Overwhelmed by realistic complexities but determined to be effective, the member narrows his range of observation, limits the definition of the scope of his responsibility, and advocates an oversimplified version of the nature of man and groups (man is rational, groups are machines). He then attempts to indoctrinate others to disbelieve in the

more obscure processes such as the unconscious, the emotive, the collective, and the implicit, all the while training them to suppress ·information and to withhold demands that would contradict his view. By being conscious of only the more obvious demands, he seeks a semblance of the competence called for by the role. As implied above, the mechanical or conflict model of groups affords him intellectual support.

4. *Self-Delusion.* The member fantasies himself as an executive because he goes through some of the appropriate motions. Although he believes that he is aware of what is going on and that his actions affect the group, in actuality he adds little to group consciousness and self-determination. Instead, he omits critical steps in the executive processes: he observes but does not correlate one observation with another; he draws inferences but fails to check them against empirical data; he dissociates the momentary situation from past history and the future; he forgets what he learns from one moment to the next; and while he may actively intervene, he takes no readings on the effect of his actions upon the group. He performs isolated segments of executive processes without tying them together into substance and consequence. And it is this which supports his delusion, for while he acts enough like an executive to suggest to himself that he is one, what he sees and does fails to matter enough to contradict his impression. Justification for his response comes not from theoretical models but from symbols and badges of position and office.

None of these four responses resolves the executive conflict; except in the most favorable conditions, they are detrimental to the development of group capabilities. In contrast, there is a response which offers promise: to begin "to learn how to learn" and to learn how to intervene. A first step in this direction is to ask questions of judgment: Of the many elements that might be known, which are *relevant*? Of the variety of formulations, which are *important*? Of the many alternative actions, which are *strategic*? [7] Judgment requires a full and intuitive familiarity with the concrete group and situation, but it is aided enormously by an effective way of thinking about groups. As an introductory guide to group dynamics for the executive, the paradigm presented in the next chapter is organized around these questions: (1) What is the purpose of a group—or, more generally, what are the order of group purposes? (2) What feedback processes and what psychological and sociological arrangements are essential for accomplishing given orders of purpose? (3) What contributions can an executive make toward creating those essentials?

[7] Needs in this direction underlie the development over the past two decades of training groups (T-Groups), of self-analytic groups, and of "sensitivity training." See again Leland P. Bradford, J. R. Gibb, and Kenneth D. Benne (eds.), *T-Group Theory and Laboratory Methods* (New York: Wiley, 1964); and Edgar H. Schein and Warren G. Bennis, *Personal and Organizational Change Through Group Methods; The Laboratory Approach* (New York: Wiley, 1965).

executive processes

a paradigm
for groups
seven

The purposes underlying the formation and operation of groups may be classified into five orders: [1] (1) immediate gratification; (2) to sustain conditions permitting gratification; (3) pursuit of a collective goal; (4) self-determination; and (5) growth.

First Order of Purpose

Individuals in groups classified according to this order seek immediate gratification of their personal needs, either through interaction with one another or, more directly, from one another. Each approaches and engages the other so as to satisfy his own needs, which may vary from sex, harm-avoidance, curiosity, warmth and safety, and relief from anxiety, to tension-release and aggression. In any case, needs are primary elements in the encounter. When they are fulfilled the purpose is accomplished, and of course when they are not, the engagement aborts.

First-order purpose is illustrated in the following instances: (a) male and female meet, copulate, then go their separate ways; (b) persons facing danger band together; (c) mother and newly-born child cling to each other; (d) villagers gather around a drummer for singing and dancing; (e) patients

---

[1] The present list is a modification of the one presented by Karl Deutsch, *The Nerves of Government* (New York: The Free Press of Glencoe, 1963), pp. 90–93. See his discussion of self-determination, integrity, and growth, to which the present paradigm is indebted, pp. 128–140; 245–254.

in a waiting-room tell one another of their problems; (f) friends of a dead person meet and mourn together.

Note that the statement of purpose is a construct. It is used by the sociologist to organize his observations of what is occurring. Its relationship to observed events is as follows: the engagement of these parties, their interaction, their conversation, their movement, and so on, are as though the purpose were, in this case, immediate gratification. The notion of purpose may or may not exist in the minds of the parties in the same form as it exists in the mind of the sociologist; it can exist on the conscious or unconscious level; it can be explicit or implicit. In any case, its service in organizing observations is useful to the observer—more useful, to be sure, when his construct is consonant with processes in the minds of group members.

Notice, as well, that our classification refers to *purposes* and not to *groups*, simply because groups often shift from one order of purpose to another, as one does from work to play.

Second Order

The purpose which guides processes of this order is to sustain contact among parties who have previously engaged one another. That is, persons who have experienced gratification (or its promise) with, or from, one another seek to continue the relationship or to reconvene it in order to satisfy needs with the same persons. This means that a second purpose—sustaining the conditions which permitted gratification—is *added* to the first rather than replacing it—a point to which we will return below. For some examples: (a) copulating creatures pair off as seasonal or permanent mates; (b) gorillas roam as a band to feed and to nest; (c) patients in the waiting-room arrange to come early next time, to have more time to talk; (d) villagers schedule a weekly dance; (e) young adolescent girls set up an exclusive club; (f) a seminar forms around a gifted teacher.

Third Order

The purpose guiding groups of this order is to pursue a collective goal. A collective goal, as stated earlier, is an idea about a desirable state of affairs for the group as a unit. Although this goal may arise out of needs, it refers to a much wider range of conditions than simply need-fulfillment. Examples of this order of purpose are commonplace: (a) father and mother teach the child; (b) one village builds a defensive wall around itself, while (c) another cuts a road to join itself to a neighboring one; (d) hunters form a joint expedition; (e) musicians form an orchestra; (f) an experimental group in the laboratory works on a problem given it by the experimenter; (g) a surgical team performs an operation.

Fourth Order

The purpose of the fourth-order group is self-determination for the group. Members seek to establish conditions which will allow them to set their own goals and pursue them, including enough freedom from external restraints, obligations, and commitments, and sufficient emancipation from past routine, habit, and tradition. They prepare themselves for a wide range of contingencies and for a change of course when they think such a change is desirable. This order or purpose is exemplified by: (a) a group of explorers moving in uncharted territory; (b) a scientific research team with promising new leads; (c) a religious sect emigrating to form an ideal com-

a paradigm for groups

munity; (d) a group of *avant-garde* artists; (e) a group of investors considering the distribution of their capital; (f) research and development teams. Notice that this order of purpose, referring to the group as a collective unit, corresponds largely to the orientation of the individual who is in the executive role.

Fifth Order

In the case of this order, their purpose is for the group to grow in capabilities and influence, or, as stated in Chapter One, to become open to wider varieties of information; capable of pursuing a wider range of goals; versatile in producing new ideas, knowledge, and techniques of value both to the group and to others; and increasingly effective in exchanging things of value with others. Certain individuals combine learning, creativity, teaching, and exchange, as in the conspicuous examples of the philosophers, the theologians, the scientists, and so on; and certain institutions do so, as in the examples of the school, the seminary, the artists' "retreats," and, in particular, the university. Yet the purpose of growth is found in less explicit and more modest form in most types of small groups: a young couple who want to raise a family; an adolescent group which sees itself as a source for new styles of language, dress, music and dance; a new firm.

These five orders of purpose are meant to be more than a list, for in our arrangement each succeeding one presumes accomplishment of the preceding one. For example, the aim to sustain connections among given individuals presumes that those persons have either been satisfied in an initial encounter, or give promise of being so; goal pursuit presumes success in holding the group together; change of goal presumes experience in reaching an initial one; and so on. The orders are cumulative. This means that the final purpose (growth) presumes the capabilities necessary to accomplish the four lower orders: (1) intermember gratification; (2) sustaining contacts among the parties; (3) reaching a common goal; and (4) altering the goal and rearranging internal and external relations in order to accomplish the new goal. We shall return to the point that the capabilities for accomplishing lower-order purposes are prerequisites for attaining higher-order ones after raising the question of what is required in order for a group to realize *any one* of the purposes.

Purpose, System Requirements, and Critical Issues

The following discussion of what a group must be and do in order to realize its purpose and to advance to a higher-order purpose is more abstract and selective than most executives (or students) would like. The excuse for its abstractness is simply that the points aim to cover a varied universe of small groups, and for its selectivity that they emphasize those structural and processual features familiar from previous sections of the book. Its purpose, to repeat, is to point to matters that are relevant, important, and strategic to the executive whose interest it is to increase group capabilities.

The first point of the thesis is that realization of any one of the purposes mentioned above and listed in the first column of Table 4 requires a complex and interdependent set of operations and arrangements. It requires feedback processes which involve connections (open network) among elements in the momentary situation. Such connections depend, in turn, upon the operation of role-systems (which open channels among elements), and these, of course, depend upon the actual entry of persons (as sources of energy, perception,

Table 4

Group Purposes, System Requirements, and Critical Issues *

Order of Purpose	Feedback Required to Accomplish Purpose — Person	Feedback Required to Accomplish Purpose — Group	Elements in Situation Relevant to Feedback (Selected)	Role-Systems Connecting Elements	Roles Persons Must Enter	Critical Issues Governing Role-Entry
1. Immediate gratification	First order	—	Ego's needs, actions; signals of needs and actions	Interaction Group emotion	Behavioral Primordial	Commitment
2. To sustain conditions for gratification	Second order (Learning)	First order	Environmental resources and limits; personal beliefs; personal and group norms	Normative	Normative	Authority
3. To pursue a collective goal	"	Second order (Learning)	Personal values and technical skills; group beliefs and values; inter-group contacts and loyalties, etc.	Technical	Instrumental	Intimacy Work
4. Group self-determination	Third order (Consciousness)	Third order (Consciousness)	Information on all elements, role-systems, etc., listed above and on inter-group obligations	Executive	Executive	Integrity
5. Growth	"	"	Increasing range in personalities, group, and context	Inter-group executive	Generative	Interchange

* The Table is cumulative; *i.e.*, as one goes down the table (from lower to higher order of purpose), all entries for preceding purposes are relevant. All entries, for example, are relevant for growth.

thought, and action) into group roles. Finally, role-entry depends upon the resolution of critical organizational problems. This interdependence is indicated by column headings in Table 4, moving from left to right.

The second point is that, as we shall see, the critical issues (listed in the right-most column) are of strategic concern to the executive. This is so because when these issues are not resolved, persons are blocked out of roles (and the group), whereas when they are resolved, persons are more willing and able to contribute their energy and thought to the group, as raw material for their development into capabilities. Consequently, success or failure in these arrangements has a disproportionately large effect upon group potential.

The third point is that as one shifts from lower to higher-order purposes (down the rows in the table), system requirements are cumulative. The previous requirements still hold, but new ones are added—such as more advanced feedback processes, connections among more elements, more advanced role-systems, new arrangements governing role-entry—and, therefore, so are additional issues of strategic concern to the executive.

The fourth point is that in the process of realizing one order of purpose, the group (its members, its culture) gains a dividend, as it were, in the form of new learning and abilities, rather than simply returning to a prior state of equilibrium. When, for example, two people find their meeting a gratifying experience, they learn more from the encounter than simply how to gain gratification. They may learn, for instance, what it would take to sustain the relationship, in which case they would be better prepared to step up to that higher-order purpose. In any case, an increment of learning beyond that required for gratification is a consequence of the encounter.

The fifth point is that this increment—this dividend—is potentially greater for higher-order purposes than for lower-order ones. A group is likely to learn more, for example, from trying to survive than from seeking transitory gratification; and, it is likely to learn more from trying to change its course to a more desirable one than by simply pursuing one already set. There is, in other words, a dynamic relation between purpose, requirements, and capabilities: though higher-order purposes are more demanding in their realization, they afford a disproportionately greater opportunity for developing capabilities. (This corresponds, of course, to the experience of the newcomer of earlier chapters who, we saw, was able to increase progressively his contribution to the group as he moved into more advanced roles.)

The sixth point is that, as far as is known, the advance of any single concrete group from one order of purpose to the next is not automatic—as though determined by an irrevocable, evolutionary, ontological program—but instead occurs through the vision and effort of group members. It is a bootstrap operation that must be imagined and engineered. Consequently, advance to a higher-order purpose is, we suggest, the second matter of strategic concern to the executive.

These six points underlie the schematic layout in Table 4, to which we return for a more detailed discussion of the first two rows and of the right-most column.

System Requirements for First-Order Purpose

In obtaining mutual gratification with, or from, one another, the various parties employ first-order feedback (as defined in Chapter One): a given party directs action toward the other(s) (a movement, a gesture, a signal, etc.), reads its effect upon the other party, redirects his action so

105

as to more nearly evoke the desired response, and eventually reads the effect of the interchange upon himself as gratifying or not. Being performed more or less simultaneously by the various parties, this order of feedback requires connections, or an open network, between the *egos* (as individual control centers), their *needs and emotions*, and their *actions* (of approach or withdrawal, expressions of frustration or satisfaction, and so on). That is, feedback can operate only if these elements, at the very least, are brought into play.

For *needs* to come into play, the person (*ego*) must be responsive to his own needs (rather than their being repressed) and attentive to the *signals of needs of others* (rather than ignoring them). If he is open to needs and their signals, then, according to our discussion in Chapter Four, he is in the primordial role: *roles*, in general, *link elements in the situation*. The primordial role links a person with his own needs and with signals of needs of others. Group emotion—a set of interrelated roles—links needs and their signals among a number of persons. Only with such linkages can the feedback processes function. Thus, entry into the primordial role, and group emotion, are requisites for those processes.

Actions are brought into play by entry into the behavioral role. The behavioral role links *actions* and *reactions* and the person (*ego*), while the interaction system links the interaction among a number of persons. This second linkage is as essential as the first for the operation of the feedback processes. In short, the role-systems of group emotion and interaction open channels among persons, needs, actions, reactions, and their signals. For such role-systems to operate, persons must enter primordial and behavioral roles.

But what, one might ask, enables the parties to deal with one another in the first place? Why should they enter role-systems with one another? Or, more specifically, what governs entry into the primordial and behavioral roles? It is this question, we suggest, that is the *critical* sociological (and executive) issue, for, to repeat, unless persons who are the primary source of both energy and thought join together on some basis, the matters of linkages and feedbacks remain academic. But if and when they do, then they may, through exploration and trial-and-error, eventually work out the kinds of role-systems which open the necessary channels. Entry into the primordial and behavioral roles is governed by the critical social arrangement we call *commitment*.

Commitment is an understanding of give-and-take among the parties. Whether explicit or implicit, it is an arrangement whereby each party agrees, in effect, to give up something for, or give something to, the other on the promise of receiving something in exchange. What is to be given may be little or much, and the balance of the exchange may never be "equal," but these details are less important than the basic question of whether or not an arrangement exists, for with it a group is possible, while without it, one is not.

Let us return to the animal world for a simple, primitive example. According to ethologists,[2] when male and female of a given species meet, there is often a rapid exchange of signals serving the function, apparently, of indicating the extent to which each party is willing and able to modify his habitual tendencies either to flee or to attack, and instead to come into close enough contact for sexual gratification. If it is true that their initial tendencies are either to attack or to flee, then to the outside observer, their coming together is circumstantial evidence of their having "made" an arrangement according

[2] See Konrad Z. Lorenz, "The Role of Aggression in Group Formation," in Bertram Schaffner (ed.), *Group Processes: Transactions of the Fourth Conference* (New York: Josiah Macy, Jr., Foundation, 1959), pp. 181–252.

a paradigm for groups

to which the fighting and fleeing responses are to be given up and, instead, sexual access granted to the other. This "arrangement," arrived at through the exchange of unambiguous signals, is a prerequisite for successful mating; it is the functional equivalent of what we mean more generally by commitment.

Commitment is essentially promissory: one gives up something with a feeling of promise, or on the promise that something will be forthcoming in return. It is precisely this willingness to give up more than one gets in immediate return (and the signaling of this willingness) that endows the relation with trust and makes it social.

To summarize, and going from left to right in the first row of Table 4, intermember gratification requires first-order feedback—action, reading effects of action, modifying actions, and so on; feedback entails an open network connecting the energy systems of persons with one another, with their needs and actions, and with signals of needs and actions. Such networks are opened when, and only when, the several members enter primordial and behavioral roles. An interaction system and group emotion are, therefore, requisites. Entry into these systems is governed by the presence or absence of a promissory social arrangement of give-and-take, called commitment.

Such an arrangement, we emphasize, is critical for the group, for without it no meaningful relation exists while with some form of arrangement persons are able to make energy, thought, and other resources available for working out the remaining requirements.

The strategic questions for the executive are: What do members want from the group? What are they prepared to give to it? What does the group want from members, and what can it give them?

Sustaining the Group
and the Issue of Authority

Let us follow the second row of Table 4 much as we have the first, in the hope that retracing once more the interdependence between *purpose, feedback, role-systems*, and *issue* will be a sufficient guide so that afterward the reader may trace the steps in the other rows while we direct attention to the other critical issues.

In sustaining a group—let us assume a continuation or repetition of conditions which have permitted gratification in the past—members: (1) observe indications from both themselves and from the external environment as to what is necessary to form a group; (2) through self-control modify or inhibit those demands for immediate gratification which might disperse the parties; and (3) regulate their interpersonal patterns of action and emotions so as to maximize in the end the chances for both group survival and personal gratification. Control processes on behalf of this *dual* purpose entail the formulation of concrete ideas about what must be done for the group to survive, and about what must be done in it to permit gratification. Such ideas, when applied to specific acts and conditions, are, as we stated in Chapter Five, *norms*. Norms are brought into play only when a plurality of members enter the normative role, for the normative role (and the normative system) links *egos*, *needs, actions*, and *realities* of the internal and external environment, with *ideas* about what should be felt and done. Entry into the normative role calls upon the person to control himself—to inhibit his desires, postpone gratification, rechannel his energy, restrain his actions, and so on—according to a set

107

of ideas (prescriptions and prohibitions) in the minds of others and himself, but at the same time not to so restrict himself that he is incapable of giving and receiving gratification.

It is at this point, of course, that the classic conflict between the individual and the group arises: the individual must relinquish personal freedom so that the group is able to coordinate itself and survive, while the group (its agents) must allow individuals sufficient freedom and access to gratification to maintain their membership, even though that freedom may endanger group survival. This opposition between individual latitude and collective coordination is, essentially, an issue of *authority*. Its resolution depends upon a moral arrangement among members, providing for an agreed-upon way of setting and modifying rules—a supraordinate set of rules for making rules. When rules are tentative, modifiable, and negotiable, then members are more likely to subject themselves to them without feeling that they jeopardize their chance for gratification, or (in the face of changing circumstances) the group's chance for survival. Fixed rules, on the other hand, lead to a variety of reactions which tend to complicate entry into the normative role: rebellion against the rules and those who symbolize them; over-controlled self-restriction; uncontrolled impulsive behavior; leaving the group; and so on.

The strategic questions for the executive are: What are the group norms? How, and by whom, are they set? Do they take into account the needs of members and the environmental realities? And, finally, what provisions is there for their negotiation and revision?

Goal-Pursuit, Intimacy, and Work

The prospect of working together toward a common goal brings people together on new and special terms. If we assume that their earlier relation was for the sake of individual gratification, we can assume that it is now oriented toward the shared idea of a goal—a goal that supersedes the individual. In order to realize the goal it may be necessary to rearrange the inter-personal relationships: those who prefer to stay apart may be brought into close contact; enemies may have to forego fighting and lovers may have to stay far enough apart to get the job done. In addition, it may call on persons to do things they have been taught not to do and to associate with those they have been taught not to associate with—to break norms and taboos. All this leads to the general point that the attempt of a number of individuals to reach a common goal tends to disrupt the existing structure of emotional and normative relations and to require a redistribution of energy, affect, and action. In this sense, the demands of entering into instrumental roles to accomplish a group goal introduces the classical conflict between self-oriented pairs (or cliques) and the group as a whole.[3] If, on the one hand, members refuse or are unable to give up or modify their primal relations, then they are held back from entering freely into the instrumental role; while on the other, if, for the sake of the goal, they detach themselves from those relations, then they sacrifice a major source of gratification. The conflict creates what we call the *intimacy* issue. It is one of two matters that govern entry into the instrumental role.

Resolution depends, we suggest, upon a social arrangement among the parties which: (1) acknowledges the distinction between affective relations and goal-pursuit (*e.g.*, to work with another does not mean that one must like the other; task involvement with another does not mean total personal involve-

[3] Philip E. Slater, "On Social Regression," *American Sociological Review* (June 1963), XXVIII: 339–364.

108

ment; and so on); (2) provides that rewards for goal-achievement are to be independent of the nature of interpersonal, affective relations (*e.g.*, enemies who are effective workers are not to be punished because of their negative relation; and, ineffective lovers are not to be rewarded for their positive relation); and (3) provides, in general, that those who work together have *the option of a variety of affective relations*, so long as they do not interfere with gratification of others, with group survival, or with collective goal-attainment. That is, a work group may be comprised of a set of affective relations varying from close to distant, from warm to cold, from positive to negative—all of which, within the limits suggested above, are negotiable by the parties concerned.

Negotiability of such a variety of interpersonal relations is the first condition that increases the likelihood of entry into the instrumental role. The second involves the arrangement for work. Discovering a common target and aiming for it presents both a possibility of success and a chance of failure. It offers the attraction of joint movement, mastery, productivity, and creativity, and as such, promises its own rewards (as workers in an artisan shop, athletes on a relay team, medics in the operating room, actors in a theatrical troop, students in a seminar, and others, often realize). At the same time, specification of a clear target means that it can be missed; or, in the case of specifying clear standards of excellence, that the product can be undesirable or worthless; and, in general, that the group can fail, and suffer from feelings of shame, incompetence, and inferiority. The second issue governing role entry is, therefore, whether the prospects for success and reward are enough to offset the chances and fears of failure. This we call the *work* issue.

Resolution of this issue depends upon a variety of conditions, three of which we emphasize. The first is a design, a plan, or a technical program which both relates one worker's activities with those of others, and links in a more or less unbroken chain their operations to the achievement of the goal. The second is a provision for differential rewards (money, goods, prestige, acclaim, deference from others, and so on) to be given according to differential contributions toward goal-achievement. The third is an arrangement whereby both the technical plan and the reward system may be modified—the plan according to discoveries, inventions, and changing environmental conditions, and the schedule of rewards according to changes both in the importance of operations and in the needs of workers. These provisions, when added to those regarding intimacy, increase the likelihood of entry into the instrumental role.

On *intimacy* the strategic questions for the executive are: How close, how distant, are members? What provision is there for rechanneling energy and feelings associated with interpersonal relations into the collective effort, while at the same time leaving options for members to engage in a variety of interpersonal relations ranging from the more detached to the most intimate? On *work*, the questions are: What provision is there for a flexible plan for reaching the goal and for a modifiable schedule of rewards for goal achievement?

Self-Determination and Integrity

Aside from the technical difficulties which might be enough to discourage the more cautious from entering the executive role (which, as implied by the fourth row of Table 4 is essential for group self-determination), the prospect of self-awareness and goal-changing raises group

109

(collective) issues which are likely to discourage even the most able and confident. We call them together the issue of *integrity*.

You will recall the suggestion in Chapter Two that groups characteristically close ranks against the outside observer and that, as a consequence, the sociologist is denied inside information unless and until he and the group develop a relationship of mutual trust. And you will recall the suggestion in Chapter Six that groups, quite beyond their conscious intentions and in the service of cohesion, resist "too much" self-knowledge. In short, the prospect of self-awareness arouses resistance. When the observer *is* an outsider, the group may simply deny him access, but the problem is not so simple when he is a fellow member. Groups, like the villagers who stone the prophet, burn the philosopher, and crucify the messiah, turn against their fellows who hold a mirror to them. The question is: How are groups able to admit a detached, objective, alien-like view of themselves (it may be positive as well as negative but, in any case, it reflects present areas of ignorance) without resenting, punishing, and expelling the one who brings it, thereby splitting the group apart?

Resolution depends upon an explicit or implicit arrangement paralleling in major respects the one between the group and the sociologist-observer. Accordingly, *access to*, and *the right to publicize*, the private, personal processes and the more sacred group process is granted only to those who show promise of becoming unconditionally committed to the group (to the executive role). In turn, those who assume a responsibility for self-awareness are granted immunity from punishment because of what they happen to discover and convey. Without such an arrangement, even those who are able to manage the technical difficulties of group self-consciousness are not likely to enter or (if they do enter) remain in the executive role.

A second issue arises from the prospect of shifting the group goal. Characteristically, we look back with special interest to the turning points in the histories of nations, families, and individuals, and with some sense of pride (and relief) when a decisive choice turns out to have been well-advised. Such interest shows how uncertain (and often how anxious and afraid) we are when major collective goals are in the process of being changed. One reason for the depth of such concern may be the common, though implicit, assumption that a group is synonymous with its goal: the *raison d'être* of a group *is* its goal (a football team *is* to win; a surgical team *is* to operate; a theater group *is* to perform; and so on). When group and goal are condensed into the same thing, it follows that to entertain an alternative goal is to doubt the legitimacy of the group as it is, to debate various alternatives is to disorient the group, and to select a new goal is to create a new group. Before groups will change their goal, they must in their culture distinguish between themselves and their present goal. The issue is subject to question from several sides: (1) To what extent can the group remain intact, its members still committed, its resources still available, its capabilities unimpaired, and its energies in reserve, while it stops its present activity in order to consider alternative goals? (2) If and when it changes its goal, to what extent can it recommit itself without impairment? (3) To what extent can it repeatedly shift directions without its members becoming afraid of losing their way, of wandering, of becoming a lost group?

Holding a group together while it considers what it is and where it might go, and while it alters directions, requires more than a social contract among members. It requires, first, a sociological conception of the group, similar to the notion of the meta-group mentioned on page 89. According to this

a paradigm for groups

notion a group is more than a goal, more than a set of rules, more than a structure of affective relations, and more than a pattern of interaction. The meta-group transcends both these sub-aspects and the momentary situation; it includes processes members are unaware of, and potentials which are yet to be realized. Such a conception, when shared by members, supports both a program for self-discovery, and the consideration of alternative goals. Beyond this, yet consonant with it, resolution depends upon a shared set of values which include humility and faith. Deutsch suggests: "To combine humility with faith, to be capable of rapid and thorough commitment without losing the openness to alternative information, and the capacity for rearrangement and possible recommitment to other goals, or to a different understanding of some of the goals previously sought—that is, perhaps, a requirement for all autonomous systems that are to have a good chance of extended survival." [4]

The strategic questions for the executive are: What is the group's conception of itself? To what extent does this conception acknowledge that the group is more than it can presently know itself to be, more than its present goal, and more than what it is currently doing? Is there humility enough to allow increasing self-consciousness, and faith enough to experiment with alternative goals? Can it both know itself and shift its directions without impairing its capabilities?

Growth and Interchange

A group's capacity to grow, as outlined in Chapter One, pages 19–22, depends upon entry of members into still another role which, after Erikson,[5] we call the *generative* role. Its functions are: (1) to explore the past and present physical, cultural, and social environment for information, ideas, designs, techniques, products, and so on, that might be valuable to the group; (2) to import selectively and to create new ideas, knowledge, designs, and the like, through recombining the new and the old, the external and the internal; and (3) to become both conscious of this creative experience and able to translate it into a communicable form so that it may be either stored for future use or made the basis for the formation of new groups. This role requires the crossing of traditional boundaries separating insiders from outsiders, one's own group from other groups. It means an expanding network of outside relations: a readiness to contact "foreigners"; to take into the group their ideas, languages, and products; and to send out (or give up) to foreigners one's own ideas, products, and even personnel. It means relinquishing group members and their contributions for the sake of creating new groups with goals that differ from one's own. It means, in short, the progressive permeation of those boundaries which ordinarily define and secure one's group, the reformation of relations with other groups, and the formation of new groups.

One reaction to such a prospect is for the group to give up its identity. The group may become xenophilic—that is, lovers of foreign or strange things— like the mountain-dwelling Arapesh, for instance, who import their *good* things (like songs, dances, and dress styles) from the neighboring beach people, and their *bad* things (such as aggression against their fellow Arapesh) from the Plainsmen who are viewed as sorcerers.[6] A second and equally defensive re-

[4] Deutsch, *The Nerves of Government*, p. 232.

[5] Erik H. Erikson, *Childhood and Society* (New York: Norton, 1950), p. 231.

[6] Margaret Mead, *Sex and Temperament in Three Societies*, in the trilogy *From the South Seas* (New York: Morrow, 1939), pp. 3–14.

111

action, of course, is to equate group identity with the boundaries themselves, and to solidify them. One's group becomes apprehensive of the consequences of external contact when (for example) consciousness of others shows them to be more desirable than oneself; when exchange of persons and products with others diminishes the distinctiveness of one's own culture; and when one's group is shown to be weak, and as a result is surrounded and incorporated by other groups.

The problem of maintaining system integrity while boundaries are being permeated and the group is becoming interdependent with other groups we call the issue of *interchange*. How is it possible for the group to increase its receptivity to new information, to expand its network of intergroup contacts, to increase the volume and variety of its imports and exports, without suffering the loss of its capabilities, its identity, and its autonomy? The issue is critical to the executive, for, if unresolved, not only will the group lose what it might have gained through contact, but it runs the danger of either dissolving into other groups, or becoming increasingly closed off from others and, as a result, becoming increasingly ethnocentric.

We suggest two conditions which, among others, help resolve the interchange issue and thereby encourage entry into the generative role. The first is an understanding *among groups* which acknowledges a *differentiated* set of boundaries, some being firm while others are permeable. One may, for instance, be inside a group physically but not an insider; one may be physically away from it but not an outsider; one may use a foreign idea without either being a foreigner or exploiting the foreigner; and one may export group culture and products without impoverishing it or being disloyal to it. Such a condition exists when several groups recognize the distinction between *physical location* and *emotional attachments*. This done, a person, like a guest, may move physically from one group to the other without having that act signify, or require, a shift of primary attachment, loyalty, and responsibility from the first to the second group. And, this done, a group, like a host, may admit the presence of an outsider without having that admission signify or require equating the outsider with other members. Persons, for instance, may marry outside and move away from the clan without giving up membership in the clan and without assuming a status comparable to the spouse in his clan. Distinguishing between the ecological and sociological boundaries enables an interchange of persons among groups which maintain their identity. A similar arrangement may cover cultural exchange, wherein the distinction is between the *source* and the *use* of information, ideas, tools, techniques, and so on, and according to which freedom to *use* is granted on the condition that the *source* not be responsible for the consequences of the use.

The second condition, upon which the first perhaps ultimately depends, is having the groups share a set of values which include what Deutsch terms "grace and generosity." Grace combines a hospitable orientation to the external world as a possible (though unpredictable) source of benefit to the group, with an acknowledgement that the group is in need of benefit.[7] Generosity combines an appreciation of one's own group as a source of things potentially valuable to others, with a readiness to translate the group's experience into words, its operations into technology, and its learning into terms that can be comprehended and used by others. Through sharing these values, the various groups are able to transcend the temporal, spatial, social, and cultural boundaries blocking interchange and growth while, at the same time, main-

[7] Deutsch, *The Nerves of the Government*, pp. 236–240.

a paradigm for groups

taining those boundaries essential for a coherent, though perhaps constantly changing, sense of collective identity.

Summary of Critical Issues

Under five headings we have reviewed the group issues (listed in the far right-hand column of Table 4) of strategic importance to the executive who aims to increase group capabilities. The way they are managed makes a disproportionately large difference to the group because they govern entry of persons into roles: when the issues are not resolved, members are blocked from the roles (and from that sector of the group), but when they are resolved, or show promise of being resolved, members' energy and mental capacities become available to the group. Questions to guide the executive's observation and assessment on the six critical issues are, in summary, as follows:

1. *Commitment.* To what extent are members prepared to give to others and to the group more than they receive in immediate return? In turn, to what extent is the group prepared to do likewise for individual members?
2. *Authority.* What provision is there both for negotiation and revision of the norms and, pending revision, for adhering to current ones?
3. *Intimacy.* What provision is there for rechanneling interpersonal affect toward collective goal achievement while at the same time leaving optional to members a wide variety of interpersonal relations?
4. *Work.* How clear and how viable are the plans for linking and coordinating effort toward achievement of the goal and for distributing the rewards of goal achievement?
5. *Integrity.* To what extent are members' relations and their values such that the group can retain its capabilities while becoming conscious of itself? To what extent are they such that it can hold together while fundamentally altering its goal?
6. *Interchange.* Are the relations with other groups, and the values shared with them, such that the several groups can benefit through the exchange of personnel, goods, techniques, ideas, beliefs, customs, and values without loss of the capacity for self-determination and collective identity?

In respect to accomplishment of a purpose of a given order, the argument is that resolution of the critical issue(s) increases the likelihood of entry into given roles and, therefore, the likelihood of the operation of role-systems. These role-systems open channels among a wider range of situational elements, thereby enabling the order of feedback processes essential for accomplishing the given order of purpose.

Dynamics of Growth

It is one thing to suggest requirements for accomplishing a purpose of a given order, and another to suggest that the requirements of higher-order purposes presume the capabilities for achieving lower-order ones (as goal pursuit presumes sustaining the group). But it is admittedly more controversial and speculative to propose how and why, and the conditions under which, a group shifts from one order of purpose to another—particularly from lower to higher, because this involves a basic alteration, a mutation as it were, in members' conception of their group. Con-

113

sequently, the intention of the following remarks is more to recommend consideration of the problem than it is to present a solution.

If one's thought on how groups shift from lower- to higher-order purposes were to be led solely by the equilibrium model (discussed on pages 15–16), then the matter would be simple: we should never expect such a shift, for according to the model, success at one level of purpose results in a return to, or toward, the previous state of the group—a state in which there is simply less tension than when trying to accomplish the purpose. For instance, persons at rest experience a need for something, orient toward one another for the purpose of fulfilling their needs, succeed in doing so, and as a result return to, or toward, a state of rest. Though the model does not claim that the system is precisely the *same* as it was in the beginning, it makes no provision for the possibility of the type of major change, the basic reconstitution, or reorientation, that occurs in a shift in order of purpose.

Less restricted is the structural-functional model of Parsons, Bales, and Shils (discussed on pages 17–18), for it provides for elementary learning. In the course of working toward the accomplishment of a given order of purpose, the group (its members) have an opportunity to learn what is and is not effective. In seeking gratification, for example, they may discover new sources and forms of gratification; in sustaining the group they may learn new modes of normative control; and in pursuing a goal they may discover new and more effective techniques. Yet this learning is within the level of a given order of purpose—an order assumed by the model. Any observed shift from one order to another must be due to factors outside the model and, if the model is of groups, outside the group. In other words, although the model provides for learning within a given orientation, there is no explicit provision for basic reorientation.

The cybernetic-growth model of Deutsch contributes positively by combining an explicit value-position (namely that growth of capabilities, in general, is an ultimate purpose of information processing systems) with the notion of group consciousness, the products of which *are* a conception of the group's purpose, an awareness of the group's potentials, and an idea of what the group's purpose might become. In our discussion the value-position and the process of developing consciousness are incorporated within the orientation of the executive. They lead him—and the sociologists who share this orientation—to ask how capabilities are related to purpose, and what might be needed for the group to advance to a higher-order purpose, with its greater opportunities for growth.

Aside from specific answers regarding concrete cases which require information about the particular circumstances, we suggest the following general proposition: Although accomplishment of a given order of purpose tends to increase the group's *potential* for advancing to the next higher order, that advance is not automatic or predetermined, but instead depends upon the initiative of a member, or members, in conceiving the new purpose, formulating it, conveying it, acting according to it, and having it generally accepted by others in the group. For example, while a mutually gratifying encounter may lead to a desire to continue the relationship, continuance must first be conceived as a possibility, and must then be proposed and accepted. *Seeing* the new possibility and then *acting* on it are relevant, important, and indeed critical to group growth: when done, the group shifts to a new purpose; when not, the group of course remains on the same level of purpose. Consequently, *the redefinition and reconstitution of group purpose according to new capabilities and opportunities is the second major strategical concern for the executive.*

114

a paradigm for groups

Table 5 presents schematically the order of progression from initial interpersonal contact to the development of capacities for group growth. Orders of purpose are listed at the head of columns, and under each are charted both success in their realization (upward arrow) and failure (downward arrow). Success or failure, we have suggested, depends upon a complex arrangement of feedback processes, open channels, and role-systems, and ultimately upon the resolution of the issues which govern role-entry. Movement from one purpose to the next (from left- to right-hand column), we are now suggesting, depends upon two conditions: (1) success in accomplishing the lower-order purpose, and (2) conceiving, conveying, and inducing members to accept, the more advanced notion as their purpose. The critical steps in the entire progression are (1) *reconstituting* the group through adding new role-systems, and (2) *reorienting* the group through the induction of a more advanced purpose. It is these which are of strategic importance to the executive.

Table 5

The Orders of Purpose
and the Cumulative Effects of Success *

1. Immediate Gratification	2. To Sustain the Group	3. To Pursue a Collective Goal	4. Self-Determination	5. Growth
				(+) Group becomes both source and recipient of new capabilities and learning
			(+) Group changes own goal and experiences accomplishment (autonomy)	
		(+) Accomplishment of goal (or promise of) experienced		(−) Group closure, or regression to lower-order purpose
	(+) Group sustained		(−) Drifting—random response to various goals, or regression to lower-order purpose	
(+) Gratification (or promise of) experienced		(−) Fragmentation, or regression to lower-order purpose		
	(−) Group disbands, or random contacts only			
(−) Frustration and dissolution				

Interpersonal contact

* (+) Purpose accomplished; (−) Purpose not accomplished.

Group Structure: Individual and Group Growth

Although the paradigm emphasizes the group, the opportunities for the development of the individual member as a person, and for group development, are of course interrelated. To indicate one facet of this relation, let us pull together several strands of our discussion. In this chapter we have suggested that accomplishment of a purpose requires the operation of a certain collection of role-systems, presented this time schematically in Table 6. In the case of growth, all six role-systems are required.

Table 6

Order of Purpose and Required Role-Systems

	1. Immediate Gratification	2. To Sustain the Group	3. To Pursue a Collective Goal	4. Self-Determination	5. Growth
Role-Systems	Interaction	Interaction	Interaction	Interaction	Interaction
Required	Group Emotion	Group Emotion	Group Emotion	Group Emotion	Group Emotion
		Normative	Normative	Normative	Normative
			Technical	Technical	Technical
				Executive	Executive
					Inter-group Executive

When a group is capable of growth—when a concrete group exhibits the operation of all systems—we call its role-structure *full-fledged*, and when a concrete group displays fewer role-systems, we call it *truncated*. For instance, a "group" with no norms is truncated at the level of interaction and group emotion, and one with a goal but without executive capabilities is truncated at the technical level. Truncation, in other words, is relative to the requirements for growth. In this respect, truncated groups are incapacitated: they do not have the apparatus for accomplishing a given purpose.

The second strand is from the earlier chapters, where it was argued that as the newcomer advances through roles (from the behavioral and primordial to the normative and on to the executive) he *needs* new conceptions of himself and the group, and new performance capabilities, and he *receives* the benefit of increased opportunities to learn (to grow), and improves the value of his contributions. Although in the beginning his role repertoire may be truncated, the more it approaches the full-fledged, the greater the potential output both to himself and to the group. Now, the same holds for the group as a whole. For a group to advance from one order of purpose to another it must acquire new capabilities: it must expand its culture, resolve new issues, and add new role-systems. However, as it does so, and as members enter these new roles, the group increases both its potential for growth, and the opportunity for its members to grow.

If these two points are true, then it follows that the potential for personal development and the potential for group growth are maximized under the same set of conditions; namely, a full-fledged role-structure with an

a paradigm for groups

option for members to participate in a full repertoire of roles. This implies that the classical conflict between the individual and the group (freedom vs. restraint) is related to the nature of role-systems that may be in operation. We should expect the conflict to be more acute when the group is severely truncated, and to become less intense, or to disappear altogether, when it becomes full-fledged and when individuals' role-repertoires become more complete. From this viewpoint, the paradigm in this chapter presents in broad outline the sociological arrangements which permit resolution of the individual/ group conflict through bilateral growth of the individual and the group.

The Paradigm and the Executive

The person who enters the executive role, we have said, faces the dilemmas of omniscience and omnipotence. There being no satisfactory way out of these dilemmas, the executive must *select* the more relevant things to become conscious of, and *choose* the more strategic course of action. All persons responsible for groups select and choose on some grounds or other. The grounds offered in the paradigm in this chapter are sociological; it aims to be general enough to give perspective both on the nature of groups and on their long-run potentials, yet specific enough to suggest what is relevant to observe and strategic to do in the momentary situation.

In respect to relevance, the paradigm recommends that instead of trying to interpret the total field of elements [as defined by $E_g = f (P \cdot G \cdot C)$], he simplify his inquiry (though still tentatively and at some peril) to such questions as: What is the order of the group's purpose? What feedback processes are and are not being employed? What role-systems are and are not operating? What psychological, social, and cultural factors either block or permit entry of persons into roles? If the group *is* operating effectively at its present level of purpose, is it possible and desirable for it to advance to a higher order? Relevance is defined not in terms of all existing causes and effects, but according to a theoretical model of group dynamics and growth. The implication is that one way out of the dilemma of omniscience is to employ (again tentatively) a working model of groups.

In respect to strategy, the recommendation is that actions be directed first toward establishing those arrangements which help resolve the six critical issues (commitment, authority, intimacy, work, integrity, and interchange), and second (and when it is desirable) toward redefining the group's order of purpose. Not only, as we have said repeatedly, do the critical issues make an emphatic difference to the group, like gateways connecting higher-energy sources with control processes, or like gates cutting them off, but *they involve personality, group, and contextual elements which are relatively responsive to conscious modification.* That is, while the executive cannot alter the basic personality of a member, he may influence his orientation to the group and increase both the amount he is willing to give the group and the amount the group is willing to give him. While he cannot modify deep-seated taboos and unconscious prohibitions, or eliminate fear and suspicion between the powerful and the weak, he may arrange for negotiation among the parties, whereby they work out rules each is willing to abide by. While he cannot change, or create at will, feelings of affection or disaffection among members, he may induce members to rechannel some of those feelings into collective and productive enterprises. While he cannot force others into self-awareness, he may enter the executive role himself and, to the degree he is effective, demonstrate its usefulness, and by this means induce the group to learn ob-

117

jectively about itself and to reorganize itself consciously. While he cannot alter environmental realities at will, he may teach that the outside world is of potential use to the group rather than simply a threat. While he cannot easily "correct" ethnocentrism, he may open channels of contact and exchange between the group and others, and between its own ideas and past or future thought in other groups. And, finally, while he cannot magically lift the group to a higher-order purpose, he may, when the time is ripe, present to it possibilities for development that it had not imagined before.

In sum, then: the executive employing the paradigm defines relevance not according to all elements in the momentary situation, but according to the place of the elements within a theoretical model; he governs his strategy of action not according to all demands of the moment, but according to whether or not they critically determine the progressive development outlined in the paradigm. And, of course, if he is true to his role. he will consciously take note of how he uses the paradigm and of how useful it is to him. As he learns its strengths and weaknesses, he will alter, modify, and improve upon it.

a paradigm for groups

emotional relations
and group growth
eight

In this chapter we shall contrast the structures of emotional relations at the two opposite poles implied in the paradigm in the previous chapter (the first where a truncated structure makes the development of a social group difficult or impossible, and the other where a full-fledged structure both permits and encourages group growth). In order to illustrate selected points between these poles, we shall sketch brief profiles of affective relations, first between authority and subordinates, and then among peers.

Two Poles of Group Formation

From the beginning of our discussion of the newcomer's experience we have assumed a person who is capable of both intellectual and emotional growth. In respect to the latter, we have assumed that his emotional commitments are "capable of expansion"—a condensed term which, when expanded itself, means that he has the capacity to go beyond the pleasure principle in his relations with others and the group (that he is able both to postpone immediate gratification of his own needs and to respond to the needs of others); that beyond adherence to his personal code, he respects the codes of others; that beyond his individual aims, he appreciates the importance of attaining a collective goal; that beyond the rewards accruing to him

119

through goal accomplishment, he is able to love other persons and to care about them as a group; and finally that beyond attachment to the group as it is, he has wishes for what it might become. From the viewpoint of sociology, expanding commitment means progressive entry into, and emotional investment in, roles on the levels described in Chapters Four, Five, and Six. From the viewpoint of the person, it means a transformation from a *narcissistic* orientation, whose aim is gratification of the self alone, to a *generative* orientation, wherein the aim is to encourage the development of the capabilities of the self, others, and the group. This is a change not unlike that which occurs as the self-centered young child grows to maturity, becomes a parent, and then comes to feel tenderness toward, and concern for, not only his own, but others' children. Such a change does not mean, of course, that the primordial feelings of love, hate, fear, and anxiety are not experienced, or that the drives of hunger, thirst, sex, and aggression are entirely repressed. Rather, it means that they are rechanneled and reapportioned as libidinal attachments to the self are given up and are diffused progressively to others, to norms, to ideas, to goals, and to the potentials for group development.

As opposite poles, the narcissistic and the generative orientations can be applied, in general, to the stance persons assume toward groups. For example, if we will return to the mode of our discussion of the sociological observer and experimenter in Chapters Two and Three, the reader will recognize that the sociologist who disassociates himself from the group, except insofar as he uses it to collect his data, is operating (as far as his relation to the group is concerned) near the narcissistic pole, and that the one who attempts to expand the range of information about groups through an exchange relationship with them is operating nearer the generative pole.

Similar to our assumption about the newcomer is the assumption that the group as a whole has the capacity of expanding its emotional commitments from the primordial purpose of gratifying elementary personal needs to other and progressively higher-order purposes. We assume that the members, taken collectively, are capable of going beyond the pleasure principle: that they are able to respond to one another's needs, respect normative ideas, appreciate the group goal, care about each other, and share wishes for what the group might become. In terms of the paradigm in the previous chapter, this means that group emotion becomes invested progressively in new levels and in new role-systems and therfore is diffused throughout the full range of group elements. Such expansion cannot occur for the group as a whole, of course, unless members (or a significant proportion of them) jointly participate in it, for it takes *joint* respect to sustain group norms, *joint* appreciation to accomplish a goal, *mutual* confidence to consider alternative goals and to change goals, and *shared* values to invest in group development.

Again we may conceive of two contrasting poles: again, the *narcissistic*, where group emotion is organized around gratification; and the *generative*, where group emotion is simultaneously diffused to the group as a whole, and mobilized around a sense of responsibility for its future. In the first case, libidinal attachment is to *selves*; in the second it is to the *idea* of creating a conflict-free group which is conducive both to individual and to group growth.

The Narcissistic Pole

When one takes into account the differences among persons in their relative size, strength, and influence, Freud's description of the primal horde (referred to in Chapter Four) approximates a "group" near the

120

narcissistic pole. The horde, it will be recalled, consists of the chief, the lesser males, and the females. The chief is omnipotent. Having begotten sons and daughters, he takes all the females to himself, prohibiting sons and all other males from sexual access to them. He claims them and protects them. This exclusive right symbolizes both his character and his relation to others: he is entirely self-oriented; "he need love no one else, he may be of a masterly nature, absolutely narcissistic, but self-confident and independent." [1] He alone possesses what is valuable; he gives no more than suits him; his omnipotence is unrestrained. In contrast, the lesser males are powerless. Deprived of sexual access, they are entirely excluded from the experience of reproduction. On the periphery of the horde, they remain infantile, sterile, autistic, and unable to rebel for fear of being destroyed by the chief. If, in Bion's terms,[2] we may attribute an underlying, basic assumption to such a "group," it is that it exists in order to fulfill the narcissistic needs and capricious wishes of the chief. In any event, all parties—sons, lesser males, females, and the chief himself—act, inter-act, and avoid action, as though this were true.

The primal horde can be interpreted as a profile of groups which have resolved none of the critical issues listed in the paradigm in the previous chapter. It is devoid of norms, of a goal, of a government, and of a social apparatus for steering. No provision is made for internal and external adjustments as protections against threat or the realities of the passage of time. Instead, members are locked in a rigid structure of primordial roles: the omnipotent chief lords over sons who, through mistrust, avoid one another; the wish to kill the chief and to steal the women is endemic, yet the fear of retaliation inhibits any fundamental change. From the viewpoint of sociology, groups at this pole are not unorganized, not amorphous, not vague masses. Instead, like the primal horde, they tend to be rigidly structured. What distinguishes them is not lack of structure, but lack of capabilities. They are, in terms of the paradigm, truncated. They are "groups" without a normative system, a technical system, an executive system, and a viable arrangement for dealing with a changing external situation. They are organized, yet incapacitated. Their principle of organization is narcissism, which in itself opposes the social arrangements necessary for resolution of the critical issues of their system.

The Generative Pole

Because the capabilities of groups near this pole provide for flexibility and variation, we can expect to find among them a wide variety of arrangements and structures—and, consequently, no simple structural model to be used by way of illustration. In order to assess their generative capacity, therefore, a test is needed, not of their form or structure, but of their viability as a total system. One such test is that of reproducibility: whether they are able to reproduce from their own ranks another full-fledged, self-sustaining group, and to do so without impairing their original capabilities. Are they able through sub-division, emigration, and the transmission of patterns, norms, ideas, techniques, and so on, to generate another group similar to themselves?

Let us imagine a group whose members visualize two equally reasonable and desirable, yet mutually exclusive, goals—for example, explorers at a fork in

---

[1] Sigmund Freud, *Group Psychology and the Analysis of the Ego* (New York: Liver-wright, 1949), p. 93.
[2] W. R. Bion, *Experiences in Groups, and Other Papers* (New York: Basic Books, 1959), pp. 93–98.

the route, or a research team that discovers a highly promising lead in the course of a tightly-planned project. One reaction, of course, is to select one alternative and disregard the other. Another is to attempt both, whereupon in the case of the explorers the group voluntarily bifurcates and pursues the two routes as separate groups which later on exchange their findings. Two groups are thus created from the original one. In general, when a group is able to bifurcate, and accomplish it without sacrificing cohesion or other original capabilities, then it approaches what we have termed the generative pole.

Questions which test a group's approach to the generative pole are as follows: *Is the group able to split into two parts, with each part then being able to develop into a full-fledged system?* If so, what is the time lag between the split and the existence of two full-fledged systems? After sub-division, to what extent is each part capable of adapting to its own circumstances, of evolving and maintaining its internal organization, of pursuing an independent goal, and of determining its own history? Do these new groups remain emotionally committed to their common origin (as kinsmen do), even though they are operationally autonomous and self-determining? Are they able to enter into and honor agreements with each other? Are they able to exchange the products of their separate operations? Do they respect the integrity of each other? Finally, is the original group able to accomplish this division without substantially impairing its own capabilities?

Whether the experimental sub-division of the group is actual or hypothetical, answers to questions such as these provide the sociologist, as well as group members themselves, with information relevant to assessing the group's capacity for growth. Negative answers reveal unresolved issues and areas of conflict; for example, "There is no second person who is able to lead another group," or, "The members are so tightly knit that they cannot get along without each other," or "The groups would become competitive, each trying to undercut the other." Positive answers, on the other hand—and particularly when obtained by an actual experimental division—attest both to the resolution of the critical issues in the paradigm, and to the capacity to grow.

Change from the narcissistic to the generative orientations appears to be a highly complex process. For the individual it is only dimly suggested by our previous discussion of the newcomer, and is a problem beyond the scope of this book. The reader will find a presentation of the major issues, conflicts, and forms of success and failure in Erikson's "Identity and the Life Cycle." [3] For the group, somewhat parallel changes are suggested, though not presented as such nor even as progressive transformations, in Redl's discussion of "Leadership and Group Emotion." [4] Selected aspects of the transformations are treated in the following sections by presenting thumbnail sketches of the types of emotional relations existing between the person in authority and his subordinates, and among peers at various points between the two poles. These brief profiles will suggest certain of the dynamic changes involved in shifting from one pole toward the other. The focal questions, both for relations between authority and subordinate, and for those among peers, are as follows: How are the parties oriented to one another emotionally? What order of emotional relationship would have to exist before the parties could be separated through group division without impairing the group? We begin with five ideal-types of authority relations.

[3] Erik H. Erikson, "Identity and the Life Cycle," in *Psychological Issues* (New York: International Universities Press, 1959), I, No. 1.

[4] Fritz Redl, "Leadership and Group Emotion," in A. Paul Hare, Edgar F. Borgatta, and Robert F. Bales (eds.), *Small Groups; Studies in Social Interaction* (New York: Knopf, 1955), pp. 86–87.

emotional relations and group growth

Types of Authority Relations

Dependent-Nurturant

Because man's survival in infancy depends upon his being fed, sheltered, and cared for by those of his kind who are larger, stronger, and more able, most persons early experience dependence upon authority. Contrary to the popular belief feelings of dependence are not restricted to infancy. Instead, they reappear in various of man's later relationships as a need and a wish. Bion, a psychiatrist treating patients in groups, reports one of its variations when he notes that on occasion members, seeming to lose conscious awareness of their individuality, interact, speak, think, and otherwise communicate as though they assumed that "the group is met in order to be sustained by a leader on whom it depends for nourishment, material and spiritual, and protection."[5] When (in contradistinction to Bion) the authority complements members by assuming that he leads *in order that* they be dependent upon him, then the relationship approaches the dependent-nurturant type.

To members the authority is perceived as kind, beneficent, sensitive to the needs of others, capable of supplying needs—in general, an inexhaustible source of gratification. Whether that which is sought be food and warmth, or whether it be information, guidance, better health, entertainment, answers to problems, ideas, a theory or a philosophy, members assume that it resides in one place alone, and that one's strategy in membership is to acquire it. In return, the leader finds supplication gratifying, for he wants to be that single source.

The bond forms with the authority caring for others and the subordinates showing their appreciation to him. This amounts to a normative relation whose contract calls for sustenance and protection on the one hand, and for compliance and appreciation on the other. Between the subordinates no comparable normative arrangement exists; instead, they are depressed because there is not enough of the leader's love to go around, and consequently are jealous and competitive. Their discontent confuses the authority and can only be interpreted as ingratitude—which of course angers him. However, since all parties know that any overt expression of either ingratitude or anger between authority and subordinates could disrupt the relationship, negative feelings between them tend to be repressed, and their recognition guarded against (the authority affords more complete care, and the subordinates show clearer signs of gratitude). Still, nothing exists to counteract jealousy among the subordinates.

Insurgent-Coercive

Redl describes an example of this type:

> [The teacher] is in charge of a group of rather problematic adolescents in a school setup which is so well regimented through an established system of suppressive rules that no one dares to rebel, because it would be too futile. These children obey their teacher under the constant application of pressure. They behave sufficiently well to keep out of trouble, but they do so grudgingly. They neither identify with the teacher nor with what he represents. Their relationship toward him—with the possible exception of a "sissy" in the class— is one of intensive hatred, of piled-up aggression which is kept from exploding only by their reality-insight.[6]

[5] Bion, *Experiences in Groups*, p. 147.
[6] Redl, "Leadership and Group Emotion," in Hare, Borgatta, and Bales (eds.), *Small Groups*, p. 80.

In the insurgent-coercive relation, each party perceives the other as an aggressor. To members the leader is not only powerful, like the chief in the primal horde, but actively and dangerously oriented toward them. They may fantasy his desire to block them, to take away their capabilities, to castrate them. In turn, the authority may imagine the group's desire to dethrone him. Although both attribute aggressive intentions to the other, and both defend themselves by aggressively restraining the other, they are each afraid of their own destructive impulses. The basic assumption, shared by both parties, is that the relation is formed in order to contain aggression.

Subordinates defend themselves by banding together, by moving underground, by initiating loyalty checks in their ranks to spot stooges or would-be traitors, by creating secret signs and codes, and so on. The trusted are selected to organize and secure the band, while active and aggressive members are pressed forward to confront the authority.

Characteristically, the authority "defends" himself against threats of rebellion by sharper surveillance, by loyalty checks of his own, and by tighter controls. As a result, the group is split into two camps, which through interaction evolve a set of rules that permit battle, yet specify its limits. By this means aggression is kept within bounds. A group so divided against itself cannot pursue a collective goal; its energies are devoted instead to an uneasy containment of aggression.

Bureaucratic

Superior and subordinate are bound together in this type by a common need to avoid the unhappiness of making mistakes. They protect themselves against feelings of guilt and shame by elaborate rules and by close adherence to them.

To subordinates, the bureaucratic superior is less a danger than he is a symbol of the righteous. Although he personifies both the rules and the safety provided by conforming to them, his presence, as the superior or the boss, arouses anxiety over mistakes that conceivably might have been made, and results in just those feelings the arrangement is designed to guard against. Confused and resentful, members vacillate between trying to keep the superior at a distance, and pressing him to be more explicit in stating precisely what they should do in order to avoid error.

Meanwhile, the superior conceives of the subordinates as being composed of two "parts": one that can be shaped into a smoothly coordinated system, and the other consisting of unpredictable impulses, alien wishes, and weaknesses, all of which produce error, confusion, deviance, and disorganization. The superior is likely to try to protect the system against this latter "part" by careful indoctrination, or by curtailing informality, or by segregating friends—yet his inability to exclude completely the unsystematic part of life frustrates and angers him. Again, this is disturbing because his anger is simply another intrusion of the disruptive segment in himself—which both arouses his guilt and increases his need for self-control. So, together the parties participate in a vicious circle kept going by a sensitivity to wrongdoing, imperfect controls, and the use of more stringent rules to minimize wrongdoing.

Idealistic

The authority in this type is devoted to an ideal, whether he be a philosopher devoted to reason, a teacher to knowledge, a statesman to peace, an artist to creation, a lawyer to justice. To others, he personifies that ideal.

124

Subordinates, as followers or disciples, admire and love the leader. He is perceived as good, able, courageous, and generous (albeit demanding). His grip on reality is firm, and he is unconflicted. Of timeless quality, his words and deeds are recorded as guides and models. Many followers seclude themselves with his works, which they scrutinize, dissect, and laboriously contemplate in an attempt to assimilate their essence into themselves. Those who do not share these intense feelings of admiration for the leader and his work and words either leave the group or are excluded from it; those who do are moved by a deep sense of solidarity.

To the leader, subordinates are apprentices, students, interns—but, too, in a deeper sense, children. He expects devotion to the ideal, and a capacity to give up personal comfort and pleasures for the sake of the ideal. He may nurture and protect, or deprive, test, and challenge, but in any case his acceptance of his "children" is conditional upon their approach to the ideal. To him, they are younger versions of himself who can be trained to carry on after separation from him; through them he can transcend himself and gain immortality.

The basic assumption is that the relation is formed to pursue the ideal. Members are graded and ranked by their approach to it. The route is often marked by tests which members must "pass." Passing is rewarded by insignias, by a title or ceremony, or by other symbols of accomplishment.

Although the *means* by which the ideal may be approached are open to debate, the *ideal*, and the logical or scientific, aesthetic or religious roots of doctrine attending it, are not open to question. Instead, they tend to be accepted as near-sacred. Freud interprets the interpersonal mechanism in this type as follows: members, having identified with the leader in what they most want to be (ego-ideal), identify with one another in what they are (egos).[7] Because the ideal of the leader is part of each of them, yet beyond immediate realization, each member acquires a measure of the quality Deutsch calls "humility"— openness to the new ideas, information, and modes of procedure.[8] Because the unrealized ideal is also collective, to the extent that means toward it are subject to debate, the group itself acquires a measure of humility.

Humility, however, stops at the ideal, for the ideal itself is not negotiable. Group formation demands commitment to the single notion personified by the authority. Alternatives which contradict the ideal are not easily imagined because they depreciate both the leader and that part of the self identified with him. Alternatives tend to be either denied or subsumed under the ideal; unconsciously, they belong outside the boundaries of the group, as part of the *not-us*. As a consequence of this pattern of identification, commitment to the idealistic type of relationship involuntarily inhibits critical evaluation of ideals in general, and therefore limits the range of the imagination in discovering new and alternative ones. In short, while the idealistic relation encourages collaboration in pursuit of a collective goal, it inhibits the examination and selection of alternative ones in terms of more general values.

Democratic

"Democracy means the power and the freedom of those controlled by law to change the law, according to agreed-upon rules—and even to change these rules; but more than that it means some kind of collective self-control over the structural mechanisms of history itself."[9] When authority and

[7] Freud, *Group Psychology and the Analysis of the Ego*, pp. 71–80.
[8] Karl Deutsch, *The Nerves of Government* (New York: The Free Press of Glencoe, 1963), pp. 229–232.
[9] C. Wright Mills, *The Sociological Imagination* (New York: Grove Press, 1961), p. 116.

125

subordinate share this power and freedom, and when they join in "collective self-control over the structural mechanisms of history," we call the relation between them "democratic."

The emotional orientation of persons in the democratic type differs from those in the types we have previously described, where the emotional attachment was either to the self, to the protection of the self, or to an ideal. In contrast, in the democratic it is to the total group—or, more accurately, to the group as it is in the process of becoming. Whereas in other types the explanatory assumptions for their existence refer to some selected sector of the situation (such as the need to be cared for, or the containment of aggression, or the accomplishment of a given ideal), the basic assumption in the democratic relationship is that the relation exists in order to create a group that can be fully identified with. The group itself is the object of emotional attachment. Since what the group becomes is determined by responses to momentary situations, both authority and subordinate, to the extent that they care about how these moments are managed, are drawn into executive roles. They are drawn into "collective self-control over the mechanisms of history itself."

In the democratic type, authority and subordinate relate to each other more nearly as partners than they do in the other types. The superior loves the group rather than an ideal; the subordinate loves the group rather than the authority. Not only do they love the same object, but this object is conceptualized as a whole which incorporates each of them as parts. Through the overarching group they are conceptually and emotionally connected with each other, and therefore are able to identify with the part each plays in respect to the whole. This enables each party to add to his own orientation the orientations, responsibilities, and functions of the other. Each acquires a dual orientation: each can think both like a superior and a subordinate. Each can take the role of the other.

Familiar properties of democratic groups are consequences of this partnership. First, *any* member may become the official head; second, headship is transitory—a subordinate ascends to authority only to return to subordination; third, the elected authority is subject to the ultimate control of subordinates, for legally he may either be given emergency powers or be removed; fourth, each party is obligated to represent the interests of the other; and fifth, each is bound by the acts of the other. The important point for our discussion is that under these conditions, persons in positions of authority and subordination are interchangeable. Through the course of actual interchange, each is trained to perform the role of the other. Given a division of the group into two parts, both leaders and subordinates are available.

Types of Peer Relations

In the previous chapter the strategic questions for assessing whether intimacy among members is effectively managed were stated as follows: How close, how distant are members? What provision is there for rechanneling energy and feelings associated with interpersonal relations into the collective effort, while at the same time leaving options for members to engage in a variety of interpersonal relations ranging from the more detached to the most intimate? The following five profiles will illustrate both the stages in the resolution of this issue, and selected points between the narcissistic and generative poles.

emotional relations and group growth

Avoiders

These are like the sons in the primal horde who need each other but are unable to help each other. Overwhelmed by a sense of deprivation, each party denies both his needs and his ineptness in satisfying them by denying the existence of the other, who is only a reminder of his own deprivation. Implicitly they agree to keep apart.

Lovers

Here we refer to a special phenomenon: the dyadic narcissistic withdrawal of lovers "all wrapped up in each other," as discussed by Slater.[10] To the exclusion of other persons and of the world of reality, the pair withdraws into itself. Each party wants to be totally loved. Seeing the biological and psychic differences between the self and the other, each needs union with the other in order to complete the self and thereby become more lovable. The attractiveness of the other—the good, the beautiful—are associated with the self and are assimilated by the self through fusion with the other.

Lovers cooperate in presenting themselves to one another for exploration, admiration, and pleasure. Unveiled are the inconsequentialities, the personal, the private, the secret—all without shame. Lovers share a need, first, to discover and then to eliminate whatever differences exist between them. While they dissolve the physical and the psychic boundaries that separate them, they shield themselves against the outside world.

Being incorporated in the pair, the lover knows not who or what he is, where he begins, nor where he ends. There is no independent point from which to think or act. He cannot separate from the other (which is a part of the self) without dividing himself in two; nor can he love a third person, or become attached to an independent thought, without inflicting some measure of cruelty on his partner. With his identity diffused within the pair, he is consigned to the dyad to the exclusion of other roles and social relations. As a consequence, the lover is not only uncertain about who he is, but has no opportunity for learning this. Instead of being oriented toward growth, lovers are, as Slater suggests, oriented toward death together.

Enemies

Enemies seek each other out. When they meet, they fight. Their wish is to square off in the heart of an arena surrounded by spectators who will cheer a champion. Often they are like the sons of a dying chief who fight over the paternal inheritance. More usually, in small groups they appear to be fighting for the right to claim that inheritance—where the inheritance is access to the group's resources of gratification: sex, esteem, promotion, prestige, deference, and worship as a hero. Enemies may share the unconscious assumption that the right of the hero belongs to the strongest, most virile, and "coolest" male. Each candidate, having staked his claim, is on the lookout for another whom he both fears and admires and whom he must defeat.

Paradoxically, in fighting for an exclusive right for obtaining something from others, enemies tend to isolate themselves from the source of what they seek. First of all, the contestants demand the right to fight without outside

[10] Philip E. Slater, "On Social Regression," *American Sociological Review* (June 1963), XXVIII: 339–364.

interference, and, second, they become preoccupied with one another's mode of attack, style of defense, and major weaknesses and strength until, in time, they become a pair. They find their level of battle and their complementary tactics. They become well matched: they become mirror images of each other. Lest they lose their identities altogether, they conjure up some mark of individual distinction, such as a viewpoint, a theory or a cause—much like medieval knights who being unidentifiable inside their armour invented pennant colors and coats of arms. Quite involuntarily, perhaps, the contestants become fused into a relationship that tends in many ways to take over control of them. Neither party can withdraw without the shame of cowardice, and any attempt to change the relationship is likely to be interpreted as simply a new tactic in fighting. Meanwhile, the group is likely to demand that they either (1) make up, (2) fight to the finish, or (3) engage in combat periodically for the vicarious pleasure of the group. The irony of enemies is that in their fight for the exclusive right to sources of gratification, they not only sacrifice their individuality and afford the group vicarious pleasure, but in the process also become pawns of the group. Some enemies resolve this impasse by giving up their claim and turning to one another as potential friends.

Collaborators

Parties in this pair join forces in pursuit of a single collective goal. Personal intimacy remains an open question—one to be answered in the course of working together. Their relation contrasts with those described above wherein the parties are defending themselves against free and open contact and where the degree of closeness and distance is fixed by the basic assumption of the relation, in the sense that avoiders must stay apart, lovers must intertwine, and enemies must fight. In these cases, tension is reduced by one type of defense or another. And the degree of closeness or distance is determined by the type of defense. Among collaborators, tension is reduced by progressive movement toward a joint goal, closeness and distance being left open to their experience together. This is to say that while collaborators are committed to a common goal, they are not committed to a given degree of intimacy.

While working toward their goal, collaborators are free to explore what the self and the other are like, and to test out the satisfactions or tensions that arise when they come closer or move further apart—and in this respect they are free to experiment with various degrees of intimacy without becoming irrevocably committed to any one state. Although some goals demand more closeness than others, the chief point is that by reason of their relationship, collaborators do not *have* to love one another, or hate one another, or fight with one another.

Because demands for intimacy among collaborators are varied and fluid, actual moves toward, away from, and against one another gain greater significance. Since such moves are voluntary—the outcome of experience rather than the result of acting out certain compulsions—they are indicative of the actual relation that exists. They provide the parties with valid information about the nature of the pair they are forming. Consequently, the degree of intimacy arrived at helps the parties clarify who and what they are as persons, and what they as a pair can do.

The boundary separating collaborators from other members is more permeable than is the one separating other pairs. Whereas avoiders, lovers, and enemies resist outside intrusion as a means of protecting their internal defenses, collaborators have no reason intrinsic to their relationship for not expanding

128

to include other persons, if and when it is clear that they are likely to help reach their goal.

There is another reason why the collaborative relation provides the individual with a wider variety of experiences than do other relations. Since immediate obligations end when goals are reached, the relations themselves tend to be transitory—and thus, instead of being locked infinitely as half of an unalterable pair, the collaborator is committed only temporarily, and may experience a series of relations, each involving both different persons and different goals. This range of experiences provides him with additional information about himself, enables him to compare partners and working relations, and, in favorable circumstances, helps him to develop his interpersonal skills. It thereby also prepares him for the later step of setting his own goals and choosing his own collaborators.

Friends

Whereas between collaborators the critical question is their ability to work together, the critical factor between friends is the placing of a high value upon respect for each other as persons. While the strength of a collaborative pair is tested by failure and frustration, the strength of friendship is tested by disappointment, in the sense that one of the parties departs from what the other wishes him to be. And while collaborators are likely to break up either because the goal is reached or because it was unreasonable, or because of incompetence, friends are likely to part because the wishes one party has for the other intrude upon the other person. By "friends," then, we mean a pair who are faithful to one another—who remain loyal to the other even though the other is or becomes other than what one wishes him to be.

A set goal is not essential for friends. They may shift into and out of the goal-seeking role; they may shift from one goal to the other; they may play at setting up goals they enjoy pursuing together. But, as we have said, goal-setting and seeking is but one of the pleasures of being together; friendship sustains itself in the absence of a goal—its *raison d'être* is the enjoyment of mutual experiences.

Besides being free of the necessity for having a set goal, friends are also free (that is, as free as can reasonably be expected) from restrictions of space, time, and personal or social compulsions. While avoiders remain apart and lovers and enemies seek contact, friends may be friends whether together or apart. After a separation, they pick up where they left off, fill one another in on what happened while they were apart and start a new phase—all on the assumption that though time, space, and events are important, they do not determine the relationship. Although enemies must fight and lovers must love, friends are free both to fight and to love, on the assumption that their relationship encompasses both. And whereas enemies distinguish themselves from one another, and lovers incorporate their differences, friends are free to be alike or different. Finally, while avoiders, lovers, and enemies erect boundaries of exclusion, friends (even more than collaborators) are free to expand: acquiring a new friend does not exclude an old one; one's friends are introduced to each other; a friend of a friend is a friend.

The upshot of our comparison of peer relations is that friendship—being free as it is from a set goal, free from restrictions of time and space, capable of incorporating both positive and negative feelings, and capable of expansion—is a prototype of the quality of socio-emotional relations which, when existing for the collectivity as a whole, enable the group to sub-divide into separate operating parts and still retain emotional commitment to their original unit.

129

Emotional Relations and Generative Capacity

In respect to emotional relations between authority and subordinate, and among peers, the profiles we have sketched suggest that a necessary condition for group division without impairment is a triangular structure wherein authority and subordinate approach what we have called the democratic type of relation, and peers approach what we have designated friendship.

In the democratic authority relation, each party is not only emotionally and intellectually capable of taking the role of the other, but operates with the understanding that his actual position is interchangeable with the other. Together the persons identify with the total group in its potentialities and assume responsibility for negotiating new procedures, new rules, and new goals. Unlike the other forms of authority relations mentioned, the democratic tends to draw members into the executive role, and is therefore better prepared to supply skilled persons to lead new, yet affiliated units.

As long as identification among peers depends upon fusion, aggressive contact, or even a set goal, group division is likely to create additional strains both within new groups and between them. These strains can be minimized only when peer relations attain the qualities of friendship and the group as a whole learns, as friends do, that it can retain members' commitment and loyalty even though members are physically separated and oriented to different goals, and belong to a different group.

Although these ideal-type relations are only two of the number of necessary conditions, we have presented them in order to invite consideration of a more general sociological question—namely: What emotional, social, and technical capabilities must a group possess, and through what processes must it go, in order to grow through the generation of new, autonomous, full-fledged, yet kindred groups? For any given group the question may be used as a guide to a clinical analysis of its capabilities, or may be answered more directly by the simple experiment of dividing the group in two and measuring the consequences of the division. Such a program of analysis and experimentation is one example of the type of research that promises to extend our scientific understanding of groups—beyond the question of how groups are structured, to the question of their capabilities; beyond the description of what groups *are*, to an understanding of what they might *become*.

emotional relations and group growth

selected references

From the following list of books, and the footnotes in the text with which it overlaps, the reader may branch out to diverse sources in a number of academic fields which are relevant to the study of groups.

For reviews of recent trends in research, see Edgar F. Borgatta, "Small Group Research," *Current Sociology* (1960), IX:173–200; and A. Paul Hare, "Interpersonal Relations in the Small Group," in Robert E. L. Faris (ed.), *Handbook of Modern Sociology* (Chicago: Rand McNally, 1964), pp. 217–271, especially pp. 217–226. This chapter also contains an excellent bibliography on small groups research.

Useful collections of professional papers ranging from theoretical formulations to laboratory studies are: Dorwin Cartwright and Alvin Zander (eds.), *Group Dynamics*, 2nd ed. (Evanston: Row, Peterson, 1960); Eleanor E. Maccoby, Theodore M. Newcomb, and Eugene L. Hartley (eds.), *Readings in Social Psychology* (New York: Holt, 1958), 3rd ed.; and A. Paul Hare, Edgar F. Borgatta, and Robert F. Bales (eds.), *Small Groups, Studies in Social Interaction* (New York: Knopf, 1955), which contains an excellent bibliography.

For examples of empirical investigations of group processes in the neighborhood, the clinic, and the laboratory, see William F. Whyte, *Street Corner Society: The Social Structure of an Italian Slum* (Chicago: University of Chicago Press, 1943); Muzafer Sherif and Carolyn W. Sherif, *Reference Groups, Exploration into Conformity and Deviation of Adolescents* (New York: Harper and Row, 1964); H. Lennard and A. Bernstein, *The Anatomy of Psychotherapy: Systems of Communication and Expectation* (New York: Columbia University Press, 1960); and William C. Schutz, *FIRO: A Three-Dimensional Theory of Interpersonal Behavior* (New York: Rinehart, 1958). For a collection and summary of laboratory studies, see A. Paul Hare, *Handbook of Small Group Research* (New York: The Free Press of Glencoe, 1962).

For a review of research methods, see Roger W. Heyns and Ronald Lippitt, "Systematic Observation Techniques," in Gardner Lindzey (ed.), *Handbook of Social Psychology*, Vol. I (Cambridge: Addison-Wesley, 1954), pp. 370–404; and for a review of more recent techniques, see Karl E. Weick, "Systematic Observation Methods," to appear in Gardner Lindzey and Elliot Aronson (eds.), *Handbook of Social Psychology*, rev. ed., forthcoming; for a discussion of problems in observation and experimentation see Leon Festinger and Daniel Katz (eds.), *Research Methods in the Behavioral Sciences* (New York: Holt, 1953).

Theoretical formulations of the small group as a social system are: George C. Homans, *The Human Group* (New York: Harcourt, Brace, 1950); Robert F. Bales, *Interaction Process Analysis: A Method for the Study of Small Groups* (Reading, Mass.: Addison-Wesley, 1950); and Talcott Parsons, Robert F. Bales, and Edward A. Shils, *Working Papers in the Theory of Action* (Glencoe, Ill.: The Free Press, 1953).

Two clear presentations of the social-psychological view of groups are John W. Thibaut and Harold H. Kelley, *The Social Psychology of Groups* (New York: Wiley, 1959); and Barry E. Collins and Harold Guetzkow, *A Social Psychology of Group Processes for Decision-Making* (New York: Wiley, 1964).

On the relevance of small group analysis to political processes, see Sidney Verba, *Small Groups and Political Behavior: A Study of Leadership* (Princeton: Princeton University Press, 1961); and James David Barber, *Power in Committees: An Experiment in the Governmental Process* (Chicago: Rand McNally, 1966).

A provocative selection of papers and an assessment of the current state of theory and research, with emphasis upon neglected areas, is contained in Warren G. Bennis, Edgar H. Schein, David E. Berlew, and Fred I. Steele, *Interpersonal Dynamics: Essays and Readings in Human Interaction* (Homewood, Ill.: Dorsey, 1964).

For an important new departure in the conception of and interpretation of the emotional and symbolic processes in groups, see Philip E. Slater, *Microcosm: Structural, Psychological and Religious Evolution in Groups* (New York: Wiley, 1966); and for a scheme for analyzing the interplay of personal and group issues, see Dorothy Stock Whitaker and Morton A. Lieberman, *Psychotherapy Through the Group Process* (New York: Atherton, 1964).

On the use of groups in training and teaching, see Leland P. Bradford, J. R. Gibb, and Kenneth D. Benne (eds.), *T-Group Theory and Laboratory Methods* (New York: Wiley, 1964); Warren G. Bennis, Kenneth D. Benne, and Robert Chin, *The Planning of Change* (New York: Holt, Rinehart and Winston, 1961); and Edgar H. Schein and Warren G. Bennis, *Personal and Organizational Change Through Group Methods: The Laboratory Approach* (New York: Wiley, 1965).

On the application of mathematical thinking and techniques, see Herbert Simon, *Models of Man: Social and Rational* (New York: Wiley, 1957); Joseph Berger, Bernard Cohen, J. Laurie Snell, and Morris Zelditch, Jr., *Types of Formalization in Small-Group Research* (Boston: Houghton Mifflin, 1962); and Joan Criswell, Herbert Solomon, and Patric Suppes (eds.), *Mathematical Methods in Small Group Processes* (Stanford: Stanford University Press, 1962).

Past issues (through 1966) of *The Journal of Abnormal and Social Psychology* are a valuable source of research reports. Major current sources include *Sociometry* and *Human Relations*. *Behavioral Science* reports the application of mathematics and computer techniques to a wide range of problems, a number of which are relevant to small groups.

index

135

index

index